OCCUPATIONAL STRESS

HEALTH AND PERFORMANCE AT WORK

Edited by

Stewart Wolf, MD
Albert J. Finestone, MD

PSG PUBLISHING COMPANY, INC.
LITTLETON, MASSACHUSETTS

Library of Congress Cataloging-in-Publication Data

Main entry under title:

Occupational stress.

  Includes bibliographies and index.
  1. Job stress—United States—Addresses, essays,
lectures. 2. Industrial hygiene—United States—
Addresses, essays, lectures. 3. Industrial safety—
United States—Addresses, essays, lectures.
4. Industry—Social aspects—United States—Addresses,
essays, lectures. I. Wolf, Stewart, 1914–
II. Finestone, Albert J. [DNLM: 1. Job Satisfaction.
2. Occupational Medicine. 3. Psychology, Industrial.
4. Stress, Psychological. WA 495 0155]
HF5548.85.025 1986   158.7   85-31941
ISBN 0-88416-484-5

Published by:
PSG PUBLISHING COMPANY, INC.
545 Great Road
Littleton, Massachusetts 01460

Printed in the United States of America

International Standard Book Number: 0-88416-484-5

Library of Congress Catalog Card Number: 85-31941

Last digit is print number: 9 8 7 6 5 4 3 2 1

CONTRIBUTORS

JOHN G. BRUHN, PhD
Professor of Preventive
  Medicine and Community
  Health, and of Human
  Ecology
University of Texas Medical
  Branch
Dean
University of Texas School for
  Allied Sciences
Galveston, Texas

BERTRAM D. DINMAN, MD,
  DSc
Vice President, Health and
  Safety
Aluminum Company of
  America
Pittsburgh, Pennsylvania

ALBERT J. FINESTONE, MD
Associate Dean for Continuing
  Medical Education
Clinical Professor of Medicine
Temple University School of
  Medicine
Philadelphia, Pennsylvania

THOMAS C. FLEMING, MD
Senior Vice President and
  Medical Director
Sudler and Hennessey, Inc.
New York, New York

MARIANNE FRANKEN-
  HAEUSER, PhD
Head, Psychology Division,
  Department of Psychiatry
  and Psychology
Professor of Psychology
Karolinska Institute
Stockholm, Sweden

BERTIL GARDELL, PhD
Professor of Social Psychology
  of Work
University of Stockholm
Stockholm, Sweden

HELEN GOODELL, BS
Research Associate Emeritus,
  Department of Neurology
Research Consultant,
  Westchester Division
Cornell–New York Hospital
  Medical Center
New York, New York

LENNART LEVI, MD
Professor of Psychosocial
  Medicine
Chairman
Laboratory for Clinical Stress
  Research
Karolinska Institute
Director of National Institute
  of Psychosocial Factors and
  Health
Stockholm, Sweden

KRISTINA ORTH-GOMÉR, PhD
Professor and Head
Unit for Social Environment
National Institute for Psycho-
social Factors and Health
Stockholm, Sweden

STEPHEN R. PERMUT, MD
Medical Director
Total Health Plus
Blue Cross Blue Shield of
Delaware
Wilmington, Delaware

FRED B. ROGERS, MD
Professor of Family Practice
and Community Health
Temple University School of
Medicine
Philadelphia, Pennsylvania

BONNIE C. SEAMONDS,
CS, MA
Consultant to Citicorp
B. Seamonds and Associates
Westport, Connecticut

GUNNAR SEVELIUS, MD
Medical Director
Lockheed Missiles and Space
Co., Inc.
Sunnyvale, California

TÖRES THEORELL, MD
Professor and Head
Unit for Health Care
National Institute for Psycho-
social Factors and Health
Stockholm, Sweden

CLINTON G. WEIMAN, MD
Senior Vice President and
Medical Director
Citibank
New York, New York

STEWART WOLF, MD
Director
Totts Gap Medical Research
Laboratories, Inc.
Professor of Medicine
Temple University School of
Medicine
Philadelphia, Pennsylvania

CONTENTS

PREFACE

The enlightened occupational physician is primarily concerned with the pursuit of health for all employees rather than merely the removal or mitigation of hazards and the management of sickness or injury.

Health care is increasingly looked upon in America as a person's right, so much so that costs seem to have been ignored. For the future, however, it is necessary to compute costs against requirements and against potential losses to the company of nonproductivity due to ill health of all sorts. Indeed, the cost of an effective health care program may appear modest against the potential waste of company funds when the services of carefully trained personnel are lost to the company through premature retirement because of illness or disillusionment. To train a skilled mechanic costs his employer several thousand dollars. The cost of preparing an executive for his responsibilities may run into the hundreds of thousands of dollars. Thus, as Robertson has pointed out,[1] protecting the lives and health of business employees has not only a humanitarian justification but also a practical financial one as well. To create and effectively accomplish a health plan suited to the future, the active involvement of management with the medical department and supervisory personnel will be required. So also will effective communication with unions and with the workers themselves.

Our American social system is founded on the work ethic. The setting of employment and daily work is, for most of us, crucial to the fulfillment of our goals and aspirations and to the realization of our potential. As most of us spend at least a third of our lives on some sort of a job, working becomes a major aspect of our way of life. Indeed, everyone either works for a living or is wholly or partially dependent on someone who does. Even the independently wealthy person is dependent for his enjoyment of life upon the goods and services provided by someone who works.

While industrial hazards are still an important problem to the health of the worker, equally important are barriers to the exercise of independent judgment and the use of individual talents. Boredom, frustration, and insecurity can not only curb productivity but can contribute to ill health.

Cotton Mather wrote:

> I will in the first place readily acknowledge that one of the worst Maladies, which a Man in any Trade, or Way of Living, can ever fall into is for a Man to be sick of his Trade. If a man has a Disaffection to the Business that he has been brought up to and must live upon, 'tis what will expose him to many and grievous Temptations and hold him in a sort of perpetual Imprisonment. Man, beg of God a heart reconciled unto thy Business, and if He has besto'd such a heart upon thee, as to take Delight in thy daily Labour, be very thankful for such a Mercy![2]

As the realization of aspirations and the fulfillment of one's potential are important components of health and well-being, a concern with occupational health becomes not only a matter for the industrialist and his medical department, but for everyone who works, irrespective of compensation and level of employment. Handicaps from disability, the prospect and the experience of retirement, as well as unemployment itself pose very special threats to our sense of worth and also to our health.

In the first half of the present century "diseases of occupation" demanded the attention of the industrial physician. Lately he has been able to shift his primary focus to the task of health maintenance. The earlier concern of physicians with plagues and epidemics of infection and the multiple hazards of the work place stimulated epidemiologic study and the emergence of public health officials and sanitary engineers. Their work with the environment had a major influence on the health of workers as well as on the population at large.

Many of today's most significant hazards to health derive from human behavior itself, for example, alcoholism, drug addicition, venereal disease, and automobile accidents. Mitigating their effects poses a special problem for industrial medical personnel and transcends the usual limits of medical practice. Thus, occupational health cannot be thought of merely as a medical specialty – it is everybody's business.

The present volume is a sequel to *Occupational Health and Mantalent Development* by Robert Collier Page, published in 1963,[3] and to a more recent volume by Wolf et al published in 1978.[4] Dr Page, who died in 1977, was a pioneer of modern occupational health. As medical director of the then Standard Oil Company of New Jersey, he emphasized a broad ecologic point of view, seeing the worker's environment not only in terms of the air he breathes and the substances he touches, but also in terms of his social milieu and the congruence of his activities in the work place with his individual aspirations, attitudes, and values. Page recognized the salubrious nature of enjoyment, satisfaction, and personal fulfillment, and the destructive effects of dissatisfaction, frustration, and failure. The task of medicine is, in Page's words, to "add life to years, rather than years to life." This book quotes freely from Page's book, with his permission and, with the permission of Charles C Thomas & Co, from the subsequent volume referred to above.[4]

The contributors to this book include an industrial psychologist and medical directors of five quite diverse American corporations: a bank, an advertising firm, an aircraft manufacturer, a defense contractor, and a basic industry. Each has shared his first-hand experience with problems of occupational stress. Research on the subject, carried out in actual work settings with employees in various types of jobs, has been described by Dr Lennart Levi and his colleagues at his institute in Stockholm. The remaining contributors are from medical schools and other health science facilities in different parts of the United States.

The editors are grateful to Helen Goodell for her help with organizing the volume and to Joy Colarusso-Lowe for her skill and patience in producing the manuscript.

The present work will not attempt to provide detailed information on industrial toxicology, already available in other texts, but will further elaborate and document the importance of personal fulfillment and job satisfaction to the health of the worker. It is intended not just for the corporate medical officer but for the student of medicine who must consider the medical impact of his patient's working life.

Stewart Wolf
Albert J. Finestone

CHAPTER 1

STRESS, SATISFACTION, AND MORALE IN RELATION TO HEALTH AND PRODUCTIVITY

JOHN G. BRUHN
STEWART WOLF

The industrial revolution has brought undreamed of creature comforts, labor-saving devices, and other material benefits to a large segment of the world's population. It has also exposed more and more people to a myriad of dangers from atmospheric and water pollution, radiation, electricity, allergies, and noise. In a variety of ways, it has wrought sweeping changes in the way of life of western civilization. Not only has technology affected the worker's health and that of his family through mechanical and chemical hazards, but more subtly, through the assembly line and other features of mass production, it has affected the worker's capacity for self-fulfillment and for the satisfaction of achievement. Such social changes as shortening of work hours and early retirement have also had their impact on health.

It is clearly in the interest of the employer to have healthy employees. Therefore, one must ask what being healthy consists of. Pericles in the fifth century BC provided a broad-ranging definition of health that warrants careful analysis. He defined health as a state of moral, mental and physical well-being which enabled crises in life to be faced with facility and grace. From the point of view of the employer then,

1

a healthy employee is one who is on hand and able to meet the challenges of the task. A state of health thus implies far more than freedom from infection or injury, or even freedom from headache, backache, or alcoholism. Health is a positive thing bespeaking action and effectiveness. The positive state of health is composed of many ingredients including that essential but elusive quality, motivation. Motivation and morale contribute to health not only by enhancing performance but also by promoting freedom from disease. Studies of the prevalence of myocardial infarction in western industrialized societies, for example, have revealed a correlation with dissatisfaction at work, working more and enjoying it less.[5,6] Not only myocardial infarction but a host of less catastrophic illnesses, such as peptic ulcer, mucous colitis, asthma, etc, which are associated with frequent attendance at the health clinic, are often related to job dissatisfaction and frustration.[7]

Motivation, according to the behavioral psychologists, can be reduced to the anticipation of reward or the desire to avoid punishment. To accept such a simplistic formulation would require an immensely broad definition of reward. Among powerful motivations of people are love and hate. Other motivations are the approval of the crowd or of peers, applause, appreciation. Particularly important is a feeling of being needed, of belonging, and a sense of accomplishment. The absence of these psychological rewards cannot only kill motivation but can actually lead to the disruption of certain of the body's regulatory processes and so to disease. There is a vast literature relating psychosocial stresses to bodily disorders, disease, and even death.[8-11]

A case in point is that of a 47-year-old lawyer who had symptoms of peptic ulcer for 14 years beginning when he had affiliated himself with a law firm. He had had a long remission during the years of World War II, and following the war he had had a severe episode of hemorrhage. There were many pertinent facts in his history. He had been born of Jewish parents who had emigrated to the United States from Russia.

His mother and father had worked hard and made extraordinary sacrifices to enable their children to have a high school and college education. The patient, the "flower" of the family, had been sent to law school, where he had led his class. Just prior to graduation and against the desire of his parents, he anglicized his name and married a Roman Catholic girl. After graduation he affiliated himself with a firm of gentile lawyers, a decision interpreted by his family as an attempt to disavow his Jewish ancestry and indentify himself as a gentile in the competitive world of big city law practice.

Before long, he became the most heavily depended-on lawyer in the office, but the senior partners failed to take him into partnership. When it seemed as if the partners could no longer escape admitting him into partnership, they employed a second Jewish lawyer. Thereupon the senior partner told the patient that he was unable to appoint him to the firm since he now had two Jewish lawyers on his staff and did not wish to show any favoritism. It was in this setting that be began to experience periodic epigastric pain relieved by food and soda. Symptoms continued until the outbreak of World War II when most of the members of the firm were called into military service. The patient, deferred because of his duodenal ulcer, had to assume the full responsibility of running the office. Despite the heavy load of work at night and on weekends, the patient welcomed this opportunity to show his capacities and was flattered by the magnitude of his responsibilities. During these years of hard work his symptoms of peptic ulcer subsided altogether. After the war when his Jewish associate returned from military service and reestablished the former state of affairs at the office, his ulcer symptoms returned to a degree more severe than before. When the senior partners still refused to admit him into partnership, he suffered a severe hemorrhage.

This patient's story illustrates that the demands of work and the burden of responsibility may be less pertinent to the precipitation of peptic ulcer than are the frustrations that go with them. The pathogenic process derives from the significance of the circumstances to the particular individual involved.[12,13]

SOCIAL REASONS FOR ILLNESS

Most industrial firms now recognize that an eager and dedicated worker is likely to be a healthy worker. Since the job situation plays an important part in the emotional nourishment of most Americans, the balance of satisfactions versus frustrations on the job becomes important to the health of the employee. Industries that have provided recreational facilities and opportunities for relaxed fellowship have taken a step in this direction, but much more is needed to make a significant impact on the health of employees. Further studies of human nature are required. Working mothers make up a substantial portion of the present-day work force. Their needs revolve around mundane family problems—how to arrange to care for a sick child or to pick up a child after school. The lives of most American men are divided into three spheres of activity. In younger years activities center on home, school, hobbies, and recreation; later the main activities are home, job, hobbies, and recreation; finally, there is retirement with heavy reliance on home, hobbies, and recreation.

PROVIDING THE INGREDIENTS OF MOTIVATION AND MORALE

Considerable frustration and disappointment at work can be tolerated if the home situation is secure, supportive, and satisfying. Conversely, a secure, supportive and satisfying work situation can often enable a person to tolerate a good deal of frustration, lack of appreciation, and disappointment in his family setting. But when both situations are insecure, trouble is likely.

Some of man's most basic needs can be satisfied by a good job in which the employee feels a commitment to the mission or an emotional attachment to the organization. Among those needs are:

1. *Need for a purpose or objective in which he can believe and to which he can devote himself.* Enthusiasm for the mission is found frequently among insurance salesmen who feel that they are performing an important social service in protecting their clients; indeed, other salesmen who believe in their products may feel, in a sense, like benefactors of their customers. Craftsmen, too, are likely to enjoy a satisfying pride in their work. Where a person's relationship to the ultimate product or service is less clear, however, special means must be undertaken to engender in employees their needed sense of purpose.

2. *Need to be needed and to feel appreciated.* Neglect of this elementary human requirement moved Thoreau to remark that most people live out their lives in quiet desperation[14] – a hyperbole, perhaps, but one that offers an important insight into human nature and a useful lesson for employers. Man not only needs something to look forward to and to work toward, but he needs to feel useful, worthy.

3. *Need to feel competent.* Contrary feelings of inferiority and self-depreciation with consequent fear of responsibility and, more frightening, of exposure often lie behind instances of alcoholism and other types of self-destructive behavior, including suicide. Jobs should fit the temperament and talents of the worker. Personnel failures may follow on the heels of promotions, for example, especially from one line of work to another, when the fit of the person for the job is not realistically taken into account.

Mr A quit school in the tenth grade, entered aircraft school and later the Navy, where he was an aviation machinist mate third class. Later he joined an aviation firm as a mechanic. After 5 years, he was promoted to inspector with a $4000 a year raise. The new job required him to make decisions as to maintenance standards and procedures, as well as the final decision as to whether an aircraft was airworthy. He found the work exhausting and worrisome. His smoking increased from one to two or three packages of cigarettes a day. He even considered returning to his father's grocery business. But there were conflicts with his father so he stayed on as inspector. Four years later, continuing in this job that he found so burdensome and lacking in satisfaction, he suffered a myocardial infarction. The company, unaware of Mr A's problems with supervision and the constant responsibility of decisions involving safety, had promoted him because of good performance in a subordinate job without inquiring into his desires and aspirations or assessing his ability to handle the increased responsibility of being an inspector.

Mr B, whose education had also stopped at high school, left his job in the retail bread business for a better paying position in an insurance firm. Because of his high productivity he earned a promotion to manager of his division. In this post the size of his income depended to a large extent on the productivity of the agents under his supervision. He soon found himself worrying over interpersonal conflicts with some of the agents, the resignation of others, and the need to train new recruits. In this setting, feeling caught between pressures from his company to produce and his difficulties with his subordinates, he suffered a myocardial infarction. He told the doctor at the time that he had been happier as an assistant manager making less but being free of the worries of supervision. Three years before, he had turned down a much bigger salary offer to become director of agencies because of the large amount of traveling required.

In our society there is a strong emphasis on "getting ahead" and "making good." Promotion, therefore, signifies recognition by others, more pay, in most cases more fringe benefits and status. While many would find satisfaction in promotion, not everyone is comfortable with added responsibilities. Unfortunately, employers may advance employees as a reward for loyalty and performance in the former job, without carefully considering the match of the person to the new post. Almost every large company provides lavish living proof of the "Peter principle" which recognizes the problem of the poor fit in stating that most people are promoted to the level of their incompetence.

It is by no means the exclusive province of the employer to attend to the basic needs outlined above. To ignore them, however, is to court poor morale and poor performance.

PROMOTING PERSONAL GROWTH

A newly recognized and only recently adopted responsibility of industry is that of helping workers grow emotionally through self-understanding as they work. In keeping with this point of view, Hershey and Blanchard[15] urged that managerial practice be geared to an employee's current level of maturity, with the overall goal of helping him to develop as a person, to require less external control, and to gain more self-control. Many approaches have been tried, including leadership workshops, and courses of various sorts.

Although the employer can help workers grow, any real progress requires individual initiative on the part of the employee himself. Whyte[16] warned against becoming so tied to organizational life and the peace of mind engendered by promises of security that any drive to be individualistic is lost. Perhaps less attention should be given to fitting the individual to the work group than fitting the work group to the individual.

A medical department that is familiar with the employees as individuals can contribute a great deal to promoting job satisfaction. Otherwise, in a society that is highly oriented toward production and economic reward, the psychological and social needs of workers may be overlooked. The purpose of occupational health and industrial health personnel should be to cultivate the attitudes and practices of management and workers alike so that work will be at once healthful and satisfying, rewarding to the worker, and productive for the organization.

CHAPTER 2

HISTORICAL PERSPECTIVE

HELEN GOODELL
STEWART WOLF
FRED B. ROGERS

As with so many aspects of medicine, the concern with occupational health begins with Hippocrates in the fifth century BC (Figure 2-1). His book *Airs, Waters, and Places,* was written as a health guide for Greek mercantile colonists who had set up trading posts in remote places.[17] It was the view of the Hippocratic physician that the characteristics of health and disease are conditioned by the external environment. Until the late nineteenth century when the germ theory took over, *Airs, Waters, and Places* was reissued as a practical guide to physicians. It stressed the importance of man's environment as a factor in disease, including physical, climatologic, and social elements, and what today is termed life style.

THE NATURE OF THE WORK AND THE WORKER

The idea that the type of work bears a relationship to the type of disease experienced was proposed 300 years ago by the great Ramazzini (Figure 2-2) in Italy.[18] Bernardino Ramazzini described in detail the diseases of people engaged in some forty types of work and advised his fellow physicians

Figure 2-1 Hippocrates (460–375 BC).

to question their patients about their occupations. In his book
De morbis artificum diatriba published in 1700, Ramazzini,
who stressed prevention rather than treatment, urging attention to the special characteristics of individual workers,
anticipated many of our present concerns in occupational
medicine. His work had little or no impact on English-
speaking countries at the time, but by present day historians
of medicine, he is acknowledged as the "father of occupational
medicine." While Ramazzini recognized that "sharp and acid
particles" in the air at the work environment of the crafts
could cause disease, he was equally concerned with the habits
and behavior of workers and with the adverse effects of other
environmental factors such as poor housing, fatigue, and
malnutrition. His belief that occupational illness was the end
result of many interactions between the worker and his

Figure 2-2 Bernardino Ramazzini (1633–1714).

environment–social, economic, cultural, philosophical, political, and religious,–presaged the current ecological view of disease.

THE NATURE AND MEANING OF EXPERIENCE

About a century after Ramazzini, another important idea took shape, namely that intellectual functions, emotions, movements of muscles, and alterations in the behavior of internal organs are a consequence of the brain's processing of sensory experience. In eighteenth century France in the midst of raging battles over the mind-body problem, a unified concept based on physiology began to develop. The central figure in this development was Pierre-Jean-Georges Cabanis, a man familiar to very few American physicians, medical students, or even medical academics.[19] His intellectual progenitor was the seventeenth century physician-philosopher John Locke who, with his predecessor, Pierre Gassendi, held that all knowledge comes through sensory experience.[20,21] Cabanis pursued the idea that thoughts and emotions, and also general somatic and visceral behavior, were responsive to life experiences perceived through the senses and processed in the brain.

PHYSICAL AND CHEMICAL HAZARDS IN THE WORKPLACE

In 1831, C. Turner Thackrah (Figure 2-3), a surgeon of Leeds, in his pioneer work, *The Effects of the Principal Arts,*

Figure 2-3 Charles Turner Thackrah (1795–1833).

Trades and Professions, and of Civic States and Habits of Living on Health and Longevity, produced the first systematic publication in Great Britain concerning industrial disease and its prevention.[22] Although he followed to some extent Ramazzini's work, Thackrah dealt with several diseases incident to trades peculiar to England. He investigated brass poisoning and illness due to dusts, and also made careful observations on special trade hazards, including bad posture in shoemakers. Also in Britain, Sir Thomas Oliver, early in the twentieth century, edited and wrote two treatises on dangerous trades and diseases of occupation,[23,24] as did Sir Leonard Erskine Hill who compiled a book on caisson sickness and the physiology of work in compressed air.[25]

In the United States, George M. Kober (Figure 2-4), a leader in American public health, introduced teaching of oc-

Figure 2-4 George M. Kober (1850–1931).

cupational medicine at Georgetown University Medical School in 1890. He also wrote an early text, *Industrial and Personal Hygiene* (1908).[26] In 1909 Harry E. Mock began the policy of medical examinations for employees at Sears, Roebuck & Co in Chicago. He noted that by that time 21 states had passed acts which had a direct bearing on the sanitation of factories. His paper, *Industrial Medicine and Surgery,* published in the *Journal of the American Medical Association* in 1919, was a landmark in the field of occupational health.[27]

The first National Congress on Occupational Disease was held in 1910 in Chicago. In that year Alice Hamilton (Figure 2-5) of the Harvard Medical School commenced her industrial hygiene career with a publication about lead poisoning.[28] A subsequent classic, *Industrial Poisons in the United States*

Figure 2-5 Alice Hamilton (1869–1970).

(1925), established Dr Hamilton as an authority on health promotion in industry.

SOCIAL AND PSYCHOLOGICAL FACTORS IN INDUSTRIAL PRODUCTIVITY

Recognition of the relevance of emotional and social factors to job performance and to health has been achieved mainly in the present century. It has led to a systematic concern for the psychological welfare of employees. Hugo Munsterberg (1863–1916), one of America's first applied psychologists, extended psychology into industry and law and wrote the first textbooks in these areas.[29] He and his colleagues studied the effects of fatigue in occupation and recommended the institution of rest periods to improve the workers' morale as well as their productivity.

Industrial accidents have been reduced greatly as a result of psychological studies. Morris S. Viteles and others found some persons to be "accident-prone", ie, they tend to have more than their expected share of accidents.[30] He found that counseling along with installing accident-proof equipment, and requiring frequent inspection of factories, reduces industrial mishaps.[31]

Employees' motives and grievances are likewise important to production. Between 1927 and 1932 the pioneering research at the Hawthorne plant (Chicago) of the Western Electric Co demonstrated the importance of skillful interviewing in diagnosis and also revealed dramatic therapeutic benefits from individual discussions and counseling.[32] A study by company officials also demonstrated that improved productivity could be achieved from groups of workers simply by a display of management's concern for their welfare. In order to enhance production they installed more intense lighting in one of the workrooms. Soon the productivity of the group exceeded that of all other groups.[33] Then it was suggested that the female employees might do even better if the walls were painted a pastel shade. That worked, too. Really interested now, management decided to test the effect of increasing the height of the workbenches by 6 in. Again productivity increased, but then it was discovered that lowering the workbenches by 6 in had the same effect. Ultimately, it became clear to the officials that what was helping these workers toward better achievement was the evidence that someone was interested in their welfare and comfort. This study caught the imagination of the industrial medical community and considerably enhanced attention to the psychological and social aspects of the workplace.

SOCIAL AND PSYCHOLOGICAL FACTORS IN HEALTH AND DISEASE

The growing interest in the relationship of psychological and social well-being to health sparked a new view of the old mind-body dilemma. An enlightened observer and philosopher of this development was Alan Gregg (Figure 2-6) who wrote in the *Harvard Medical Alumni Bulletin* in 1936:

> The totality that is a human being has been divided for study into parts and systems; one cannot decry the method, but one is not obliged to remain satisfied with its results alone.
>
> What brings and keeps our several organs and numerous functions in harmony and federation? And what has medicine to say of the facile separation of "mind" from "body"? What makes an individual what the word implies—not divided? The need for more knowledge here is of an excruciating obviousness. But more than mere need, there is a foreshadowing of changes to come. Psychiatry is astir, neurophysiology is crescent, neurosurgery flourishes, and a star still hangs over the cradle of endocrinology.
>
> Contributions from other fields are to seek from psychology, cultural anthropology, sociology, and philosophy as well as from chemistry and physics and internal medicine to resolve the dichotomy of mind and body left us by Descartes.[34]

Figure 2-6 Alan Gregg (1890–1957).

Fortunately, as Director of the Medical Board of the Rockefeller Foundation, Gregg was able to be more than philosopher. Through his recommendations, the foundation provided support for individuals and institutions bent on developing further the study of psychological and social factors in medicine.

Shortly before the United States entered World War II, the Macy Foundation and the National Research Council had financed an ecumenical movement among medical scientists, physicians, and psychiatrists that led to the founding of the American Psychosomatic Society (then called the American Society for Research in Psychosomatic Problems).

The society, whose birth was greeted with great enthusiasm and probably exaggerated hopes for ultimate enlightenment, experienced a stormy and troubled infancy, childhood, and adolescence. Psychoanalysis was sweeping toward the apex of its popularity in this country and abroad while at the same time almost nothing was known about what was going on in the brain. Norbert Wiener's milestone book on cybernetics[35] had yet to appear and Warren McCulloch had yet to propose his models of feedback circuits in the CNS with their versatile excitatory and inhibitory capabilities.[36] Thereafter, developments in what came to be known as neuroscience occurred rapidly, especially knowledge of the distribution of brain circuits and the way they work. Some psychic states were found to be associated with a predominance or deficiency of certain neurotransmitter chemicals in various parts of the brain. The growing anatomical, chemical, and pharmacologic knowledge of mechanisms was supplemented by evidence from animals and humans adduced through stereotaxic stimulation of the brain, conditioning, and clinical observations, and experiments with stress interviews showing that forebrain circuits concerned with the recognition and interpretation of life experiences are capable of influencing virtually all, if not all, regulatory mechanisms in the body.[37] Thus, tangible physiologic and biochemical explanations were emerging to explain the favorable effects on the worker of interest and appreciation on the part of his supervisor and the unfavorable physical and behavioral consequences of disappointment and frustration in, as well as outside, the workplace could begin to be understood in terms of underlying neurohumoral perturbations.

EVOLUTION OF INDUSTRIAL MEDICINE

In 1948, Dr Robert Kehoe's Kettering Laboratory for Industrial Health at the University of Cincinnati initiated with Dr Donald Ross of the Department of Psychiatry a training program for industrial physicians in the psychological aspects of occupational health. Out of this grew Ross's book, *Practical Psychiatry for Industrial Physicians,* published in 1956.[38]

In his *History of Medicine* (1954), Ralph H. Major wrote:

> The rapid growth of industrial plants, notably in the United States, has posed new problems unknown to the previous generation of physicians. The problems of installing proper safeguards for health, of proper lighting, of supervision of diets, of correct sanitation, and of the prevention as well as the care of the increasing number of industrial accidents have led to the creation of a new medical specialty—that of industrial medicine. The modern industrial plants maintain on their staffs sanitary engineers, trained dieticians and are equipped with excellent hospitals, furnished with the latest X-ray and surgical equipment under the direction of skilled physicians and surgeons as well as well-trained nurses.[39]

Occupational medicine now has its own specialty boards.

SOCIAL IMPLICATIONS

In 1971, the then Secretary of Health, Education, and Welfare, Elliot L. Richardson (Figure 2-7), established a commission to examine work as a fundamental social institution in America. The study was carried out under contract with the WE Upjohn Institute, Kalamazoo, Mich, for Employment Research.

After a thorough review of the existing literature, Richardson summed up the study with a quotation from Albert Camus:

> Without work all life goes rotten. But when work is soulless life stifles and dies"[40] .... Because work is central to the lives of so many Americans, [wrote Richardson] either the absence of work or employment in meaningless work is creating an increasingly intolerable situation. The human costs of this state of affairs are manifested in work alienation, alcoholism, drug addiction and other symptoms of poor mental

Figure 2-7 Elliot L. Richardson (born 1920).

health. . . . Industry is paying for its continued attachment to Tayloristic practices through lower worker productivity and high rates of sabotage, absenteeism and turnover. Unions are paying through the faltering loyalty of a young membership that is increasingly concerned about the apparent disinterest of its leadership in problems of job satisfaction.[41]

Taylorism refers to the teachings of Frederick Winslow Taylor whose 1911 book, *Principles of Scientific Management,* recommended that work tasks be greatly simplified, fragmented, and compartmentalized and also placed under continuous supervision.[42]

In Richardson's view treating workers better without changing the nature of their jobs is no cure for the harmful effects of Taylorism. The report of his special task force adds:

> Many industrial engineers feel that gains in productivity will come about mainly through the introduction of new technology. They feel that tapping the latent productivity of workers is a relatively unimportant part of the whole question of productivity. This is the attitude that was behind the construction of the General Motors auto plant in Lordstown, Ohio, the newest and most "efficient" auto plant in America. Early in 1972, workers there went on strike over the pace of the line and the robot-like tasks that they were asked to perform. This even highlights the role of the human element in productivity: What does the employer gain by having a "perfectly efficient" assembly line if his workers are out on strike because of the oppressive and dehumanized experience of working on the "perfect" line? As the costs of absenteeism, wildcat strikes, turnover, and industrial sabotage become an increasingly significant part of the cost of doing business, it is becoming clear that the current concept of industrial efficiency conveniently but mistakenly ignores the social half of the question.[42]

In the wake of what appears to be the unsettled fate of Taylorism, there has emerged evidence that high morale, self esteem, a sense of importance and power, and recognition and appreciation by others are conducive to health and longevity. The concept extends another step the more negative concept of 40 or more years ago that social and emotional stress are contributory to bodily disorders and diseases.

The anthropologist Sula Benet, studying the Abkhasians of southern Russia, found among these hard-working people extraordinary hardihood and longevity.[43] She wrote: "Both the Soviet medical profession and the Abkhasians agree that their work habits have a great deal to do with their longevity. The doctors say that the way Abkhasians work helps the vital organs function optimally. The Abkhasians say, 'without rest, a man cannot work; without work, the rest does not give you any benefit.'" Concerning their social structure, she noted: "The high degree of integration in their lives, the sense of group identity that gives each individual an unshaken feeling of personal security and continuity, permits the Abkhasians as a people to adapt themselves—yet preserve themselves—to the changing conditions imposed by the larger society in which they live." Dr Benet describes the Abkhasians as "a life loving, optimistic people." Concerning the place of the elderly, she writes: "Unlike so many very old dependent people in the United States who feel they are a burden to themselves and their families [the Abkhasians] enjoy the prospect of continued life . . . in a culture which so highly values continuity in its traditions."[43]

A very similar set of circumstances was noted much closer to home in Roseto, an Italian-American town in eastern Pennsylvania originally settled in 1882. In the early 1960s Roseto was found to have a remarkably low death rate from myocardial infarction despite a prevalence of the usually accepted risk factors closely similar to those in neighboring communities where coronary deaths occurred at twice Roseto's rate.[44] The striking feature of Roseto was its social structure. Because the Italians were initially shunned by the mainly Anglo-Saxon inhabitants of the region, their natural cohesiveness was actually accentuated. Not only were the family units extremely close and mutually supportive, but so was the community as a whole, so that there was essentially no poverty and virtually no crime. The male-female relationships in Roseto were those of the "old country" with the man the undisputed head of the household. Moreover, the elderly were respected and listened to. Both men and women lived to an old age, and indeed the death rate among women was slightly greater than that among men, leading to the unusual presence in the community of a few more widowers than widows. Sadly, as with new generations further removed from the influences of the old country, family ties in Roseto began to weaken and the attitude of mutual support in the community was less evident. At the same time the Rosetans began to lose their remarkable longevity and their relative immunity from myocardial infarction. As home and community life became less emotionally satisfying, the Rosetans sought emotional nourishment at work. Looking more broadly at the American work scene, a study commissioned by the Secretary of Health, Education, and Welfare and published in 1973 found "the strongest predictor of longevity was work satisfaction. The second best predictor—overall happiness."[45]

Kobassa et al,[46] studying management personnel undergoing stressful experience, noted vulnerability to disease varied widely from person to person and was least among those judged by independently administered tests as "hardy" personalities, capable of adjusting to change and hardships.

Irrespective of differences in vulnerability, a strong sense of group identity, a feeling of being needed and valued, and a sense of accomplishment are important requirements of individuals in a healthy society and are worth cultivating in the workplace. The process of healthy adaptation for man involves his elaborate use of language and other symbols and reflects his special sensitivity about his place in the eyes of other men. As a tribal creature with a long period of development, he depends for his very existence on the aid, support, and encouragement of other humans. He lives his life so much in contact with others, and he is so deeply concerned about their expectations of him, that perhaps his greatest need is for their approval and acceptance.

It is folly to ignore these basic characteristics of human beings in their work lives, especially now that the support of close-knit families has weakened and traditional institutions such as the church no longer envelop whole communities. The next historical development must be general recognition that a healthy industrial society provides for the human needs and aspirations of its workers. And perhaps the captains of industry will learn that to lead people is a more appropriate aim than just to manage them.

ACKNOWLEDGMENT

The figures in this chapter are reproduced with the permission of the Historical Collections of the College of Physicians of Philadelphia.

Section II:
Bodily Mechanisms
That Mediate Stress

CHAPTER **3**

CENTRAL NEURAL CIRCUITRY INVOLVED IN EMOTIONAL STRESS

STEWART WOLF

Stresses at the workplace are, of course, universal and inevitable. Most involve not so much exhausting physical demands but what are perceived as unreasonable attitudes and unfair practices of subordinates, coworkers or superiors. It is not the stresses themselves that lead to trouble, but rather an insufficiency of balancing forces that provide social support, satisfaction, and a sense of achievement. As pointed out in chapter 1, the resultant of psychological and social equations involving human relations depends on the balance between the positive satisfying and fulfilling elements of a job and such negative features as frustration, boredom, and a feeling of being unappreciated. The compensating rewards may seem subtle but they provide for very familiar human needs such as a sense of personal dignity and importance, a feeling of being recognized as a person, and of being appreciated. The vaunted labor relations of Japanese and some Scandinavian industries are based on attempts to satisfy such universal human needs and to provide, as well, the very important element of job security.

Symptom-producing bodily and behavioral disturbances brought on by psychologically and socially stressful circumstances are largely the consequence of changes in neural and neurohormonal regulatory mechanisms which normally

24

maintain homeostasis but may respond with major deviations to signals from circuits in the frontal lobes of the brain that interpret life experience. The resulting bodily responses are shaped, then, by the *meaning* of an experience which is influenced in turn by individual characteristics that are partly inborn and partly acquired. Afferent impulses conveyed to the brain in the course of day-to-day living from situations that challenge, threaten, or disrupt in some way a person's sense of satisfaction and well-being are translated into patterns of response. The patterns, affected by a host of accompanying circumstances and contingencies, are characteristic for each individual. Thus, it is not the stimulus situation itself, but its peculiar individual significance that determines the pattern of response. Responses are further modulated by one's prevailing state of tension or relaxation, one's mood and outlook on the world at the time, as well as by cyclic rises and falls in a multitude of regulatory functions over a 24-hour day, the diurnal and circadian rhythms. Attempts to measure an emotion will not help explain the reactions since emotion is not the stimulus, but like the associated bodily disturbance, it is a response to the event, circumstance or experience. The outcome is determined by numerous excitatory and inhibitory interactions involved in the central processing of afferent signals from the experience itself.

The efferent pathways used in responding to symbolic stimuli, the words and gestures that can reward or punish, are the same ones that mediate adjustments to the ordinary tasks of daily living, eg, eating and exercise. Gastric acid secretion is enhanced during anger and resentment in the same way it is during hunger or while devouring a meal.[47] Running calls forth the same tachycardia and accelerated breathing that accompanies anxiety when a person is not moving at all. Automatic homeostatic adjustments such as the acceleration of heart rate in response to exercise are triggered at relatively low levels of neural integration in cord, medulla, and midbrain. Tachycardia occurring in anticipation of exercise, however, as in those preparing for a race, and the tachycardia of anxiety, involve neural structures at a higher level of integration in the frontal lobes where neuronal circuits consciously or unconsciously "interpret" the afferent information stemming from the sights, sounds, smells, and other aspects of one's surroundings.

Responses to meaningful experiences formulated in the forebrain may preempt those developed at lower levels of integration. The arrangement is not strictly hierarchical, however, as shown by Manning.[48] He and others have identified interactions among several processing regions in the brain. Thus, the old way of explaining the functions of the brain in terms of centers and levels has given way to a concept of back-and-forth traffic, interactions among several cerebral structures involving a large number of facilitatory and inhibitory association neurons which process afferent information and shape efferent responses.

In the vast network of the brain, neurons in the efferent outflow that are responsible for adaptive behavior are numbered in the millions. Neurons in the afferent inflow—those that either sense the environment or the state of things within—are numbered in the tens to hundreds of millions, while the processing neurons in the brain—those responsible for decision making and the formulation of responses—are numbered in the tens of billions (Figure 3-1). It is important to bear in mind that bodily responses to stressful circumstances need not be accompanied by conscious awareness of the emotional significance of the circumstances. Indeed, depending on the path taken by the forebrain impulses and the participation of the inhibitory circuits, the stress response may occur without any conscious experience of emotion at all. The formulation of behavioral responses to experience involves a vast complex of neuronal transactions among afferent pathways and distribution centers, the limbic areas, the frontal cortex, the cerebellum, the midbrain reticular formation, the hypothalamus, and the brainstem efferent nuclei. The endocrine regulators of homeostasis, once thought to operate

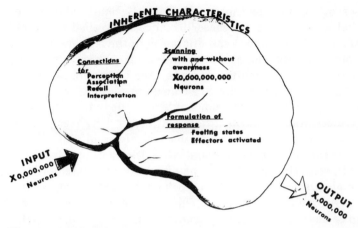

Figure 3-1 Numbers of input, output, and processing neurons concerned with perception, interpretation and response.

more or less independently of the brain, are now known to be subject ultimately to neurohumors secreted in the region of the hypothalamus. As neuropeptides, they travel via a local venous portal system to the anterior pituitary where they govern the release of the several tropic hormones which in turn control the glands of internal secretion scattered throughout the body.

Regulatory peptides have also been identified in the brain outside the hypothalamus, in ever increasing numbers. Most are also found in other tissues, most prominently the gut and kidney. Their functions have not been fully worked out as yet, but clearly there is a need to revise traditional concepts of how the brain works.

NEW KNOWLEDGE OF AUTONOMIC CIRCUITRY

Traditional views of the relationship between autonomic and somatic nerves have already been revised because of observations such as those of Hoff and Greene[49] who showed that stimulation of the sensorimotor cortex to elicit movement of a leg also produced vasodilatation in the leg muscles. The autonomically mediated vasodilatation occurred in response to the cortical stimulus even when the leg was paralyzed by curare. Thanks to technical advances in staining and in stimulating and recording from single neurons in the CNS, sympathetic and parasympathetic pathways, long classified as separate, are now known to share richly ramifying connections throughout the cord and brain. Interacting extensively with somatic neurons, autonomic pathways contribute to a single system that governs all behavior, visceral and somatic.

At one time autonomic effector functions were thought to be distinct because the structures they supply are capable of automatic responses. Voluntary control, then, was thought to be exercised only over somatically innervated structures. On the contrary, voluntary control of the bladder was observed by Denny-Brown and Robertson[50] and confirmed by ingenious studies in humans by Lapides.[51] Lapides showed that voluntary micturition does not require the involvement of skeletal muscles, even the external urethral sphincter, but is dependent solely on the detrusor muscle of the bladder, a structure totally innervated by autonomic neurons. This work and later studies using biofeedback and other therapeutic maneuvers have laid to rest the idea that visceral activity cannot be voluntarily controlled. On the other hand it is well known, but had been largely overlooked, that the automatic function of respiration is regulated through the somatic innervation of the diaphragm and thoracic musculature. Thus autonomic does not necessarily imply automatic. Neither do automatic mechanisms necessarily require autonomic innervation.

Another misconception held that autonomic nerves were part of a largely peripheral, phylogenetically primitive system concerned mainly with the regulation of body temperature, and cardiovascular, digestive, and other basic functions.

According to the pioneering studies of Gaskell[52] and Langley and Anderson[53] 100 years ago, the regulation of these and other visceral functions was thought to involve necessarily antagonistic actions of sympathetic and parasympathetic nerves. Despite strong evidence to the contrary, until recently this concept and that of Eppinger and Hess,[54] that the neurons in each of the nerve trunks are homogeneous and, when activated, discharge en masse, have stoutly resisted change. The old ideas had received some support from studies involving section of vagal and sympathetic trunks that interrupt all afferent and efferent fibers. Such measures, of course, made it impossible to identify messages from neurons that might be individually activated or inhibited while mediating discrete and differing functions. Now, thanks to data from single unit recording, it is abundantly clear that autonomic neurons are fired individually and separately in patterns appropriate to specific local tasks. Moreover, selected sympathetic and parasympathetic neurons may act in concert and not necessarily in opposition. Important demonstrations of the central integration of autonomic function have been achieved by electrical stimulation in the brain.

As early as 1875 Danilewski recorded changes in heart rate upon stimulation of the cerebral cortex.[55] Shortly after the turn of the century Karplus and Kreidl elicited cardiovascular effects by stimulation in the hypothalamus.[56] More recent evidence from elegantly localized stimulation in hypothalamic, limbic, frontal, and cerebellar sites has revealed discrete and clearly patterned responses involving not only reciprocal activity of sympathetic and parasympathetic innervation, but synergistic behavior as well, in which elements of both participate in the response. Gunn et al[57] found that stereotaxic stimulation in the region of the nucleus of the tractus solitarius of the dog resulted in apnea, bradycardia, and blood pressure elevation (Figure 3-2). These are the characteristic features of the dive or oxygen-conserving reflex and involve coordinated discharges in both sympathetic and

30

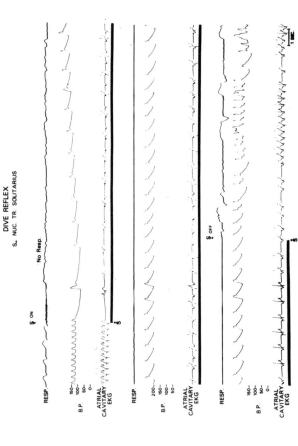

Figure 3-2 Effects of stimulation in a command area. (Reproduced with permission from Gunn et al.[56])

parasympathetic neurons.[58] Thus, stimulation of a small "command" area elicited a complex and widespread response involving specific autonomically and somatically innervated structures, the heart, the arteries, and the muscles of respiration. The technique of neural stimulation has been adapted to pharmacologic inquiry through the use of micropipettes inserted into the brain through which various neuroeffector chemicals can be brought into contact with a small collection of brain cells.

Walter Cannon's extensive investigations of intact animals dramatized the role of the autonomic and especially of the sympathetic nervous system. They led him to conclude that sympathetic discharges were mainly useful in life-threatening emergencies that people only rarely face today.[11] Therefore, he believed that to modern man the significance of sympathetic responses was mainly atavistic. His inferences were based on experiments in which his animals were required to react to potentially catastrophic situations. For example, the cornered cat was made to face a large and vicious dog. The cat's pupils dilated, his fur stood on end, his blood pressure rose, his blood clotted more readily, his bladder and colon contracted, his gastric juice ceased flowing, he arched his back, he bared his teeth and hissed. The work of later investigators has shown that such generalized autonomic and somatic discharges, although operative in major stress situations, are not characteristic of ordinary coping behavior in the face of the usual threats and challenges of daily life. In adaptation to ordinary life situations, responses are limited and discrete. Such visceral disturbances seem to occur in a variety of threatening circumstances, even in fairly disparate situations, in a fashion characteristic to the individual. For example, when faced with a domestic crisis with failure on the job, or having been passed over for a promotion, one person may develop elevated arterial blood pressure, another an asthmatic attack, while another may experience a flare-up of the symptoms of peptic ulcer. Each of these organ disturbances is autonomically innervated but each reflects discrete activation of a special set of effector neurons.

DETERMINANTS OF SYMPTOMS AND DISEASE

Beyond consideration of the anatomical structures and biochemical mechanisms involved, the proposition that bodily illness may stem more or less directly from neural processes concerned with the formulation and fulfillment of purposes has eluded general understanding, partly because of the persistence of outworn concepts relating to the genesis of symptoms and disease. The meaningless distinction between "organic" and "functional," for example, has served only to confuse. All diseases are at once functional-organic in the sense that they are manifested by a disturbance in function of some organ of the body with or without associated structural change or tissue damage. In considerations of etiology, data on mechanism have often been mistaken for cause. Thus, the discovery of a biochemical abnormality in the brain may clarify a mechanism in schizophrenia or depression, but not necessarily a cause.

Individual susceptibility or vulnerability to stressful circumstances that elicit pathophysiologic mechanisms, significant disturbances in general, or visceral behavior amounting to illness or disease, depends on a host of intervening factors including parental influences, past experience in the development of self-confidence, and acquired coping skills. Among these and other determinants, genetic influences must be of the first order of importance and, indeed, we are learning rapidly of more and more disorders that have major genetic determinants. The penetrance, or the actual manifestation of genetic proclivities may depend in turn on environmental and developmental factors. Moreover, the attitudes and emotional life of the patient may to some extent determine penetrance. Neither attempts to delineate a personality profile characteristic of the various disease states thought to be related to emotional stress, nor efforts to isolate a characteristic or "nuclear" emotional conflict have been very fruitful. Nevertheless, an individual's psychological "set" seems related in some way to his pattern of organ functioning.

The best data relating to "specificity" have come from a study of attitudes.[58] An *attitude* is interpreted broadly as the way an individual interprets his position vis-à-vis a certain situation. Most people have a characteristic Weltanschauung, or way of looking at life; perhaps more precisely, a way of reacting when cornered or seriously threatened. The gambler takes a risk, the cautious person becomes more cautious, the fighter fights, and the fleer flees. The patient with migraine meets challenging circumstances by doing things longer than, harder than, and better than his neighbor. The alcoholic meets challenges by disengaging himself from responsibility. There are a multitude of such patterns. When they are highly developed within us, as was indecisiveness in Hamlet, and when they are indiscriminantly used, they may contain the seeds of our ultimate destruction. Difficulty may arise when the pattern is strained, ie, when too much is demanded of it; or frustrated, as when some circumstance blocks its use; or when it is altogether inappropriate to the solution of the problem at hand. The forces that balance these proclivities and tend to support constructive life adjustment have to do with providing for the human needs discussed at the beginning of this chapter. Perhaps the most favored employee from this point of view is the great orchestra conductor, well known for his good health and long life. Orchestra conductors regularly experience demands on their creative aesthetic and intellectual powers. They also have the feeling of being needed, even of being indispensable; they have power in their control over a large orchestra and they enjoy the approbation, applause, and support of their audience. To a substantial degree then, they may exemplify how health equates with high morale and satisfaction in work.

CHAPTER 4

NEUROHUMORAL MEDIATORS OF EMOTIONAL STRESS

ALBERT J. FINESTONE

Norman Cousins, former editor of the *Saturday Review,* described in his book, *Anatomy of an Illness,* how he mobilized positive emotions, particularly laughter, to recover from a possible collagen vascular disease which his physicians felt had an unfavorable outlook.[60] A summary of his book appeared as a special article in the *New England Journal of Medicine.*[61] More recently, he has written another book entitled, *The Healing Heart, Antidotes to Panic and Helplessness* which emphasizes the importance of a positive mental attitude in recovering from serious illnesses such as heart disease.[62] Although Cousins has certainly popularized this notion, particularly to the lay public, unfortunately, too many physicians are unaware of this important association between the emotions and disease. Sir William Osler, years ago, stated, "Care more particularly for the individual patient than for the special features of the disease."[63] In this chapter some of the mechanisms through which emotionally stressful experiences are translated into physiologic responses will be discussed in hopes that the physician may intervene to ward off excessive or inappropriate responses that can result in pathology. Effective intervention will require understanding and sometimes altering the occupational stress. At other times, pharmacologic or psychotherapeutic approaches will be required. In any case, the physician who understands the basic pathophysiologic problem will be best able to undertake therapy.

Early in this century the physiologist Walter B. Cannon, in landmark experiments, demonstrated that the adrenal medulla could be activated by psychologic stimuli, frequently of an emergency nature, resulting in the secretion of epinephrine.[64] In the 1930s Cannon and his collaborators also discovered a substance produced at sympathetic nerve endings which resembled but was distinct from epinephrine. He named it sympathin. When it was later chemically identified by von Euler, its name was changed to norepinephrine. As a neurotransmitter, norepinephrine mediates discrete sympathetic effects that are confined to the structures affected by the specific neurons that are activated. After performing its very localized synaptic function, the norepinephrine is partly reabsorbed into the preganglionic nerve terminal and partly destroyed by local enzyme action. Very little, if any, gains access to the general circulation from interneuronal synapses, although at effector terminals on vascular smooth muscle an appreciable amount of norepinephrine reaches the bloodstream.

In contrast, when the adrenal medulla is stimulated its catecholamine products, consisting mainly of epinephrine and to a lesser extent norepinephrine, gain access to all body structures through the general circulation. Thus, the widespread "fight-or-flight" responses described by Cannon are subserved. When stress-related responses are mediated predominantly by activation of the adrenal medulla they can be monitored by measuring catechol excretion in the urine or its concentration in the blood. The more localized the discrete neuronally mediated responses are, the less likely they are to be reflected in blood or urine.

Much information on the multiple types of effector neurons contained in sympathetic trunks has evolved from the discovery of vasodilator effects of sympathetic stimulation.

Sympathetic nerves were long thought to affect blood vessels via vasoconstrictor neurons only, despite the fact that Sir Henry Dale had adduced evidence in the early part of the twentieth century that sympathetic nerve trunks contained vasodilator as well as vasoconstrictor fibers.[65] Dale's important observation remained an isolated finding for nearly 50 years until Uvnas and other workers actually traced out a sympathetic vasodilator system involving acetylcholine as the postganglionic neurotransmitter. The later landmark discovery of separate α- and β-adrenergic receptors established that norepinephrine is capable of either vasoconstriction or vasodilatation, depending on the nature of the receptor encountered.[66] The adrenergic receptors that determine the differential effects of catechols are protein molecules located within the plasma membrane of the target cells. The target cells, responsive to either circulating catechols or to synaptic connections with postganglionic sympathetic nerves, are located in the heart and vessels where hemodynamic adjustments are made and in such visceral structures as the spleen, liver, gastrointestinal (GI) tract, kidney, and pancreas where they regulate a myriad of biochemical and metabolic adaptations.[67-68]

The shared responsibilities of the endocrine chromaffin cells of the adrenal medulla, which itself is subject to its own sympathetic nerve supply, and the neurotransmitter function of norepinephrine secreted at sympathetic nerve endings throughout the body are often difficult to sort out.[69-71]

Although sympathetic innervation to some extent governs the other glands of internal secretion, activation of the adrenal cortex, the thyroid, and gonads depends primarily on tropic hormones secreted into the bloodstream by the pituitary gland. As pointed out in the previous chapter, the tropic hormones are, in turn, controlled by peptides from the hypothalamic area of the brain.

NEUROHUMORAL MECHANISMS IN
BODILY DISEASES

Afferent impulses from stressful life experiences are integrated in the reticular formation in the thalamus of the brain and interpreted in the frontal lobes. Ultimately, the hypothalamus shapes the efferent response through autonomic and neuroendocrine pathways. One of the most studied neuroendocrine systems involves the pituitary control over the release of adrenocorticotropic hormone (ACTH) and its influence on the cells of the adrenal cortex. Corticotropin releasing factor (CRF) from the hypothalamus reaches the pituitary gland through the local portal blood vessels. The released ACTH travels through the bloodstream to the adrenal gland where it triggers the release of cortisol, the final response to stress of this particular system. Normally the plasma level of cortisol, through a negative feedback mechanism, is maintained within a physiologic range. During stress, however, the cortisol concentration may rise beyond the usual range. As cortisol is necessary for survival in a stressful situation, patients with a cortisol deficiency, such as Addison's disease, are at high risk in stressful situations. One of the major functions of cortisol is to regulate cellular metabolism through the process of gluconeogenesis. Cortisol, in this circumstance, mobilizes amino acids from muscle and connective tissue to synthesize glucose. Therefore, in the short term, cortisol can increase energy supplies. However, over a long period of time cortisol mobilizes amino acids from connective tissue and muscles and therefore breaks down structural protein. This will ultimately result in failure of clotting, loss of muscle mass, and fractures. Therefore, in the short term cortisol has a homeostatic function while in the long term its catabolic function produces pathology.

Cortisol also exerts a paradoxical effect. It stabilizes plasma membranes so as to decrease their permeability. This has a beneficial short-term effect in preventing loss of fluids from the circulatory system and, therefore, helps maintain blood pressure and blood volume. However, by inhibiting the response to inflammation, cortisol prevents the body from coping with disease and infections may result as a longer term consequence. Cortisol may induce euphoria and, especially during prolonged administration, even psychotic behavior.

Other hormones involved in responses to stress include prolactin, growth hormone, insulin, testosterone, and luteinizing hormone (LH) as well as several more recently identified peptides.

A large number of regulatory peptides have been shown to be widely distributed in the nervous system, GI tract, and other tissues. These small molecules, when released from one cell, can modify the activity of neighboring or even relatively distant cells through appropriate receptors.[72] These intercellular messengers are known to include thyrotropin release factors, LH-releasing factor, corticotropin releasing factor, and growth hormone releasing factor as well as several others including β-endorphin. Table 4-1 lists the peptides found in the brain by chemical or immunologic identification methods.

Like other regulatory peptides, endorphins have been found not only in the brain, but in the gut and in the adrenal gland as well. These endogenous opioid peptides may provide an explanation of the observation that persons in acutely stressful situations are not as aware of pain as they would be without acute stress. Rapid progress in this area has developed since the detection of opiate receptor molecules that serve as specific recognition sites and as cellular mediators of opiate action.

The effects of the various hormones and other chemical regulators are actualized at the target cell level through a chain of events that begins with binding to a specific receptor either in the cell as with steroids or triiodothyronine (T_3), or on its membrane as with insulin or catecholamines. Recep-

Table 4-1
Peptides Found in the Brain by Chemical
or Immunologic Identification Methods

Thyrotropin-releasing factor	Metenkephalin and leuenkephalin
Luteinizing hormone–releasing factor	Neurotensin
Somatostatin-14	Substance P
Somatostatin-28	Bradykinin
Corticotropin-releasing factor	Bombesin
Growth hormone–releasing factor	Angiotensin II
Adrenocorticotrophic hormone (ACTH)	Glucagon
Prolactin	Gastrin
Thyrotropin	Motilin
Growth hormone	Secretin
α-Melanocyte-stimulating hormone	Gastric inhibitory polypeptide
Oxytocin	Vasoactive intestinal peptide (VIP)
Vasopressin	Cholecystokinin
β-Endorphin	Calcitonin gene-related peptide
Dynorphins	Carnosine

tor function has been well studied in the case of epinephrine's effect on skeletal muscle as shown in Figure 4-1.

The complex regulatory process involved in stress responses has recently been reviewed by Axelrod and Reisine.[73] Snyder[74] has summarized what is known of brain receptors for neurotransmitters and drugs that influence behavior.

Long before the discovery of the elegant and intricate mechanisms that mediate responses to troublesome life experiences, clinical studies had documented the bodily effects

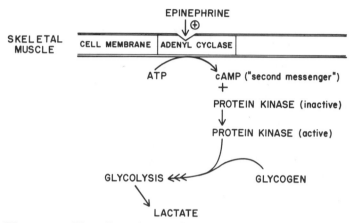

Figure 4-1 The effect of epinephrine on skeletal muscle.

of stress. More than 150 years ago, William Beaumont[75] observed the stressful environmental events on the functioning of the stomach of a man suffering from a gastric fistula. The nature of the effects was studied extensively in the experimental observations of Wolf and Wolff on a fistulous subject.[12] They were able to discern distinct patterns of gastric behavior in association with anxiety and anger as distinct from fear and depression. They also documented measurable changes in gastric acid secretion, motility, and blood flow in response to placebos.[12,76] Recent studies have suggested that regulatory peptides found in the GI tract may be involved in functional digestive disorders by acting through the enteric nervous system in the gut wall and its connections with the brain and spinal cord.[77]

There are in hypertension multiple possible psychophysiologic pathways to be activated in response to stress, including elevated cardiac output due to β-adrenergic stimulation, increased peripheral resistance or renal artery constriction attributable to α-adrenergic activity, changes in renin release, or salt and water metabolism by way of a variety of neural and hormonal mechanisms.

Sympathetically induced vasoconstriction has been a prominent putative culprit since Kottke et al[78] produced hypertension in animals by stimulating the sympathetic supply of the kidney exclusive of the adrenals. Frohlich and Pfeffer[79] have recently summarized the evidence.

Even social isolation and understimulation may give rise to stress-induced disorders in the elderly. Arnetz et al[80] recently reported psychoendocrine effects in a group of lonely and inactive elderly subjects.

Among endocrine diseases, hyperthyroidism has been thought to be related to emotional stress. Most endocrinologists who have wide experience with Graves' disease feel that such a relationship exists. The mechanism was initially attributed to increased thyroid stimulating hormone (TSH) secretion, but TSH was found to be low in untreated Graves' disease. A more likely explanation now implicates corticotropin releasing hormone, thus activating the ACTH-cortisol axis with ultimate effects on supressor T lymphocytes and immune surveillance. There is experimental evidence that stress can reduce immune surveillance and allow for the development of autoimmune diseases, perhaps including Graves' disease.[81]

There are other fascinating developments regarding the influence of brain and behavior on the immune system.[82] Considerable experimental data support the inference that psychosocial factors may modify host resistance to infection. A similar statement may be made about neoplastic disease also being influenced by psychosocial factors through the immune process. There is strong support from experiments in animals that hypothalamic lesions can alter the immune response. The mechanism is unclear at the present, but it may be actuated by autonomic and neuroendocrine pathways. In humans, T cell function has been shown to be significantly depressed after bereavement.[83-85]

The immune response is chiefly elicited by the two major classes of lymphocytes, the T and B lymphocytes. T lymphocytes mature in the thymus and are involved in cell-mediated responses, whereas B lymphocytes from the bone marrow provide the circulating antibodies. Adrenocorticosteroids and other hormones including catecholamines can influence the immune response and may participate in stress-induced immune disorders.

The most immediately fatal consequences of emotional stress stem from disruptions of cardiac rhythm. The efferent autonomic nerves that affect intra-cardiac conduction and thereby predispose to arrhythmias are responsive in reflex fashion to signals from local myocardial disturbances and are also susceptible to activation by impulses descending from the forebrain. Thereby they mediate the effects of psychosocial stress. There is some suggestion that such adverse effects may be blocked or greatly moderated by positive psychological influences, notably by strong social supports as in Roseto, for example, an emotionally cohesive Italian-American community in eastern Pennsylvania.[44]

Factors that influence the mechanisms that may precipitate sudden death are highly relevant to the occupational physician and are dealt with in detail in some of the chapters that follow.

Section III: Etiologic Significance of the Workplace, the Work, and the Worker

The chapters that follow deal mainly with symptoms and diseases that are attributable to or intensified by circumstances of adjustment to life experience, especially in the workplace. Among conditions that may be seriously affected by situational stresses are the consequences of bodily injury and the problem of rehabilitation therefrom, especially those concerned with financial compensation.

The usual difficulties of evaluating the person's capacity to work are vastly multiplied by the intervention of the factor of economic compensation and its consequent effects on motivation. Apart from problems of motivation, however, much confusion is traceable to concern over the elusive distinction between "functional" and "organic" and to the conflicting concepts of psychogenesis. Traditionally, occupational physicians have relied on anatomical changes to indicate legitimate disability. This criterion falls far short of what is needed since, on the one hand anatomical lesions can be self-inflicted, and on the other there are numerous fatal disorders in which gross or histologic anatomical changes cannot be demonstrated.

Some disabilities are directly traceable to an injury. Others are merely precipitated by the event of injury and are primarily due to the fragile and often precarious previous adjustment of the person. Such people may be thought comparable to the marginal producer in industry. This important condition is discussed in chapter 18 with examples.

A further illustrative case is that of a 60-year-old proprietor of a typewriter repair shop in a community that contained a large university. The man's car was struck from behind with comparatively little force while he was making a delivery. Nevertheless, he acquired an intense and unrelenting occipital headache that prevented his continuing to run his business. In the judgment of the orthopedist there was insufficient trauma to have produced a whiplash injury, and he so testified in court. The patient, however, was clearly incapacitated. He and his wife had been barely keeping enough customers for their business to stay afloat in the face of competition from a new typewriter repair company started by aggressive young people. During the period of several days devoted to the medical work-up and evaluation of his injury and damage to his car, it had been necessary to close the store. Consequently, calls for repairs went to the new company instead, and many regular customers were lost. By the time litigation was completed, the patient had not only lost his case but his business as well, and he was deep in a reactive depression with persisting headaches. In retrospect, it would be difficult to say that the automobile accident had no part in his headaches or his depression. Such an experience would not have produced the same effect in most men. But this individual, a marginal producer in every sense, was peculiarly susceptible to such perturbation.

Hinkle has studied the significance of social and educational background in susceptibility to illness.[86] The subjects were 139 managerial employees in one large corporation. They ranged in age from 22 to 31 years, worked in comparable environments, and earned closely similar salaries. Fifty-five of the subjects (group C) were recent college graduates hired directly as managers. The remaining 84 subjects (group H) were high school graduates who had risen from the ranks to their managerial positions. The two groups of men were compared in terms of the relative amounts and kinds of illnesses each had experienced. The group H men had had more new illnesses of many kinds during the period of observation. They also had a significantly greater amount of chronic illnesses, acne, constipation, vasomotor rhinitis, and dental caries; there were also more instances of arthritis, bronchitis, and symptoms of anxiety and tension. They had more impairments resulting from previous diseases: scars, absent teeth, and asymptomatic hemorrhoids. The "risk of death" estimated from acturarial tables containing physical characteristics known to be statistically predictive of longevity, small as it was, was nevertheless ten times higher in the H group of men than in the C group.

The H group men displayed a greater number of signs commonly considered to be prognostic of later cardiovascular disease. More of them had blood pressure higher than 140 mmHg systolic or 90 mmHg diastolic on readings obtained under standard conditions. More of them were overweight; more had depression of T-waves and ST segments in precordial leads, as observed in the ECG; and more had early evidence of arteriosclerosis in the eyegrounds.

Family histories of arteriosclerotic illness in the two groups did not differ. Neither did their diets, although the H group ate smaller breakfasts and more between meals. They also smoked more. These differences, however, could hardly explain the striking differences in health between the two groups. The important differences appeared to relate to social challenges.

Despite the similarity of job characteristics and physical and social evironments, notable differences existed between the two groups in past experiences and present life situations. The group H men had worked as blue-collar laborers for a number of years after high school graduation before attaining their present managerial positions. Even during the 1-year period of observation, the group H men had been presented more challenges, threats, and demands than had the group C men. They had married earlier and had more dependents. They had more domestic, financial, and interpersonal difficulties. Some had extra jobs, many were taking vocational training, and some were attending college at night. Thus, at the cost of exposure to a great quantity and variety of challenges, the group H subjects were "getting ahead in the world" while the group C subjects could be said, from a social point of view, merely to be continuing at the level from which they had started. Later, Hinkle and associates extended the study to 270,000 men employed by the Bell Telephone Co.[86] They found that episodes of illness and death from coronary heart disease were significantly more numerous among high school than among college graduates.

Epidemiologic data such as these suggest that healthy living and working depend on a complex interaction of factors including genetic, environmental, social, and, to an important extent, those factors that direct one's general behavior and style of life. How a company doctor can expect to enter this complex algebraic equation with factors that can tip the balance toward health is suggested in chapters 15 through 19.

Stewart Wolf
Albert J. Finestone

CHAPTER 5

COMMON AND GRAVE DISORDERS IDENTIFIED WITH OCCUPATIONAL STRESS

STEWART WOLF

The most frequent disorders responsible for absence from work and visits to "sick call" are respiratory, gastrointestinal (GI) and musculoskeletal. If common colds, flu, and bronchitis are eliminated from consideration, GI complaints predominate.[87] Peptic ulcer was previously thought of as an occupational disease among journalists, advertising executives, and taxi drivers—all highly competitive activities prominently affected by the pressure of time. The chronic diarrhea or alternating constipation and diarrhea of an irritable colon are also commonly encountered in the workplace. Beyond this there are a host of less well-defined symptom complexes which include vague epigastric discomfort with occasional nausea, "gas" and what the patient considers insufficient bowel evacuation in terms of frequency, quantity, or character of the content.

Allergies, presumed and real, are also common, especially vasomotor rhinitis and itching of the skin. Frequently, GI complaints are attributed by the patient to allergies. Musculoskeletal symptoms including aching and stiffness of the neck, back, and extremities are often referred to by the patients as arthritis. Relatively few of these patients will be found to have actual arthritis, rheumatoid or osteoarthritis; most will be suffering from the sustained skeletal muscle contraction that accompanies emotional tension.

Headache is the third category of various common complaints of employees. The most frequent—muscle tension headaches—reflect skeletal muscle disturbance comparable to that responsible for aches and pains in the muscles of the spine and extremities. Muscle tension headaches are commonly associated with emotional tension which may not be obvious. Migraine headaches with their almost universally associated perfectionistic attitudes and behavior are commonly encountered among the accounting staff and the best of the administrative assistants and secretaries. Apart from the variety of symptomatic disturbances usually referred to as functional, there are also flagrant manifestations of anxiety, phobias, hysterical loss of function, and depression.

Other stress-related disturbances with more or less grave physical consequences include, for example, cardiac arrhythmias, angina pectoris, and myocardial infarction, as well as alcohol abuse and accidents. Some forms of cancer, although related primarily to industrial toxins, have been considered by certain investigators to be accentuated by, if not attributable to, situational stresses.

CARDIOVASCULAR DISORDERS

The possible contribution of occupational stresses to the pathogenesis of coronary atherosclerosis, myocardial infarction, and sudden arrhythmic death is today receiving considerable attention in the courts as well as in the clinics. The three conditions should be considered separate because, although they often accompany one another, there is not a direct correlation between either the presence or absence of coronary atheroma, its extent or location, and either myocardial infarction or sudden arrhythmic death.

al stimuli → physical disorder

Coronary Atherosclerosis

The evidence linking atherosclerosis with emotional stress is fragmentary but intriguing. Animals subjected to confinement and other stresses have been shown to develop atherosclerosis at an accelerated rate.[88-89] Several studies in humans have shown transitory increases in serum cholesterol in association with emotionally stressful events.[90-94] Whether or not emotional stress contributes to the development of atherosclerosis in man, however, remains to be determined.

Coronary Artery Constriction

Contractile activity of the coronary arteries and its consequences have received a great deal of attention recently since techniques have become available to visualize the behavior of the coronary vessels in man in vivo. Fifty years ago, however, there was ample direct evidence of coronary constriction from the work of the great French surgeon and physiologist, René Leriche, a successor to the chair of Magendie and Claude Bernard at the Collège de France. Leriche summarized his work as follows:

> From tonus to vasoconstriction, that is to physiological hypertonia, from vasoconstriction to spasm, there is no borderline. One passes from one state to the other without transition and it is the effects rather than the thing itself which makes for differentiations. Between physiology and pathology there is no threshold. Even with perfect conservation of the arterial structure, the spasm, at a distance, has grave pathological effects, it causes pain, produces fragmented or diffuse necroses; last but not least it gives rise to capillary and arterial obliteration at the periphery of the system.[95]

At about the same time Leriche made his observations, Hochrein, in a careful autopsy study, documented the presence of myocardial infarcts in the absence of coronary atheroma.[96]

It is now widely accepted that prolonged coronary constrictions with or without underlying atheroma may result in angina pectoris, myocardial infarction, and/or sudden death.

In the presence of atherosclerosis, any constriction of a coronary vessel is likely to impair circulation more than it would in the absence of the atheromatous lesion. In fact, localized arterial constrictions have been shown to occur frequently at the site of atheromas.[97] Moreover, it is likely that thromboses may be initiated at the site of arteriosclerotic lesions without associated arterial constrictions. Furthermore, if coronary vessels are stiffened or partially occluded by atheromas, the vasodilatation required to increase myocardial oxygen delivery during exercise may not be adequate and consequently blood flow to the myocardial cells may be deficient. Thus, in the clinical manifestations of coronary disease, atherosclerosis alone may be a sufficient cause of angina pectoris or myocardial infarction or, perhaps more often, atherosclerosis may act as a contributory rather than a fundamental factor.

Sudden Death

Potentially fatal cardiac arrhythmias are for the most part the result of local reflexes set off by stimulation of afferent endings in the myocardium by local chemical changes consequent upon partial deprivation of blood flow in the heart muscle. Also, after relaxation of a coronary spasm, the sudden flow of fresh blood may produce a reflex disturbance in the rhythm of the heart beat that is potentially fatal. In addition, there is abundant evidence that central autonomic nerves that govern and may disrupt cardiac rhythm and conduction are also responsive to neural impulses from central circuits, including areas of the frontal lobes that interpret life experience. Thus, potentially fatal cardiac arrhythmias have been observed in man in response to sudden fright or frustration and even chronic anxiety and depression.

Coronary Risk Factors

The problem for the industrial physician is to sort out the significance of various contributory factors that in concert may bring about the serious cardiac disturbances discussed above. Genetic influences are likely to be fundamental determinants since there is often very prominent family clustering of myocardial infarction and sudden death. Habits, smoking, and possibly diet and lack of exercise may be contributory as may the coexistence of other diseases such as diabetes and hypertension. Temperament and behavioral patterns have also been shown to be highly pertinent to coronary disease.[97-100] It is probably not possible to assign a quantitative value to each of these risk factors but it is fairly certain that chronic frustration, discouragement, and depression associated with problems in the workplace can make a significant contribution to the pathogenic process. Individual susceptibility appears to be determined to a large extent by a particular coping style, identified as type A behavior by Rosenmann et al[97] and as the Sisyphus reaction by Wolf.[100] Both groups of workers began their studies in the mid 1950s independently of one another, and arrived at a closely similar description of the coronary-prone person which largely confirmed the impressions of earlier observers such as Von Dusch[98] and Osler.[99] Rosenmann et al made an extensive study of employees of several large West Coast corporations and were ultimately able to identify susceptibility to coronary disease in advance of the event by their behavioral criteria: a tense, alert, and confident appearance; strong voice, clipped, rapid, and emphatic speech, laconic answers; evidences of hostility, aggressiveness, and impatience; and frequent sighing during questioning.[97] Sisyphus, king of Corinth who was condemned to the lower world where he had to roll up hill a huge marble block, which as soon as it reached the top always rolled down again, was the model for Wolf's interpretation of coronary-prone behavior, a striving against real or imagined odds and, irrespective of the outcome, an inability to relax and enjoy the satisfaction of achievement.[100]

Arterial Hypertension and Stroke

The pathogenesis of essential hypertension continues to elude clear understanding but recently accumulated evidence has strengthened an old view that an initial more or less sustained arteriolar constriction is brought about through central neural regulatory mechanisms in response to situational stresses.[101] Hypertension has been thought to be related to unresolved and unexpressed frustrations and resentments developed in or accentuated by experiences in the workplace. Studies of blood pressure changes in employees working at high strain and low strain jobs are described in chapter 8.

It is probably unnecessary to point out the well-known association between hypertension and stroke. The timing of a stroke, whether in the presence of hypertension or normal arterial pressure, has been related to especially troublesome or even catastrophic situations in and out of the workplace.

The physician responsible for the health problems in a corporation encounters a mix of patients and diseases which do not differ greatly from those that face the physician in his private office. The first task is to diagnose and understand, if possible, the basis of the patient's complaints. To achieve this understanding, a thorough and perceptive medical history is the doctor's most powerful device. A long and costly exercise in diagnostic screening may reveal less and explain less than a penetrating history. To understand the contribution of psychological and social factors, the history is indispensable and will be dealt with in detail in chapter 16.

ALCOHOL ABUSE

Alcoholism is not considered an occupational disease but it is extremely common in industry and in the nation at large. It is probable that at least 80% of the nation's 4 million alcoholics are employed. The disease often goes unrecognized but is nevertheless immensely destructive to the problem drinker himself as well as to the productivity and the morale of his company. Alcoholism may be suspected in frequent absentees and in those prone to accidents. Bacon has estimated that 1500 fatal accidents at work each year are attributable to alcohol.[102] The vast problem of alcohol abuse among employees is dealt with in chapter 10.

ACCIDENTS

There seems to be little doubt that a small percentage of the population is responsible for the largest number of accidents. This finding has been confirmed in the industrial setting as well as in the general population. It has led to a concept of accident proneness related to a particular personality type. Helen Flanders Dunbar[103] described the accident-prone individual as impulsive, resentful of authority, impatient, and unable to defer gratification. Unconscious motivations may include revenge on the one hand or self-punishment for guilt on the other.

The consequences of industrial accidents cannot be understood with reference only to the nature of the bodily injury. An understanding of the person involved is also essential as noted in chapter 9.

CHAPTER 6

THE CHARACTERISTICS OF THE WORKPLACE AND THE NATURE OF ITS SOCIAL DEMANDS

LENNART LEVI
MARIANNE FRANKENHAEUSER
BERTIL GARDELL

Common denominators in the etiology of stress-related ill health flow from either a discrepancy between one's needs and the environmental possibilities for their satisfaction, one's resources for control, and the demands of the environment, or one's expectations and one's perception of the situation.[104–105]

PROBLEMS RELATED TO WORKING LIFE

Discussions of occupational stress often tend to omit physical environmental factors, in spite of the fact that such factors can influence the worker not only physically and chemically (eg, direct effects on the brain by organic solvents)[106] but also psychosocially. The latter effects can be secondary to the distress caused by, say, odors, glare, noise, extremes of temperature and humidity, etc. They can also be due to the worker's awareness, suspicion, or fear that he is exposed to life-threatening chemical hazards or to accident risks. Thus, eg, organic solvents can influence the human brain directly, whatever the worker's awareness, feelings, and beliefs. They can also influence him more indirectly, secondary to the unpleasantness of their smell. Thirdly, they can affect him because he may know of or suspect that the exposure may be harmful to him.[107]

Real life conditions usually imply a combination of many exposures. These might become superimposed on each other in an additive way or synergistically. The straw that breaks the camel's back may therefore be a rather trivial environmental factor that comes on top of a very considerable preexisting environmental load. Unfortunately, very little is known of the net effects of such combined exposures.

With regard to psychosocial stressors in the work environment, evidence exists to support the assumption that a number of properties of systems design and job content are critical not only with regard to satisfaction but also for health.[108-116]

1. Quantitative overload, ie, too much to do, time pressure, repetitious work flow in combination with one-sided job demands and high demands on attention. This is to a great extent the typical feature of mass-production technology and routinized office work.

2. Qualitative underload, ie, too narrow and one-sided job content, lack of stimulus variation, no demands on creativity or problem-solving, or low opportunities for social interaction. These jobs seem to become more common with automation and increased use of computers in both offices and manufacturing, even though there may be instances of the opposite.

3. Lack of control, especially in relation to work pace and working methods.

4. Lack of social support, at home and from fellow workers.

Very often several of these characteristics appear together and have a joint effect on health and well-being. A representative sample of the male Swedish labor force has been examined with respect to symptoms of depression, excessive fatigue, cardiovascular disease, and mortality. The workers whose jobs were characterized by heavy loads together with

low control over the work situation were represented dispro-
portionately on all these symptom variables. The least probability for illness and death was found among groups with
moderate loads combined with high control over the work
situation.[117-119]

Briefly, then, evidence exists that work stress may be
problematic in two different ways: first, there may be a direct
relation between certain objective conditions at work, physiologic and psychological stress, and ill health. Second, certain
stress conditions may create fatigue and/or passivity in individuals and thus make it more difficult for them to actively
involve themselves in changing those working conditions —
including physical and chemical risk factors — that may be
detrimental to health. This latter aspect is especially relevant
when interest focuses on ill-health prevention on the systems
level.

As pointed out by Gardell,[120] Wilensky,[121] and others, the
ill effects of mass-production technology include alienation
of the worker not just during working hours, but with a spill-
over to leisure time. An increase in apathy may grow out of
this dissatisfaction, resulting in a decreased willingness of
the worker to take part in activities outside work.

Frankenhaeuser[122] emphasizes "speed of unwinding"
after work as a key determinant of the total load to which
workers are exposed. From a psychophysiologic viewpoint it
seems reasonable that the speed with which a person unwinds
will influence the wear on his or her biological system. Hence,
the speed of unwinding is also likely to influence the extent
to which stress at work is carried over into leisure
time.[122-123]

There are large interindividual differences in the temporal pattern of psychophysiologic and psychoendocrine stress
responses. Experimental results indicate that so-called rapid
epinephrine decreasers, those whose stress-related rise in
serum or urinary concentration of epinephrine fall rapidly,
tend to be psychologically better balanced and more efficient

in achievement situations than "slow epinephrine decreasers."[124] An equally important finding is that the time of unwinding varies predictably with the individual's state of general well-being. Thus, in a group of industrial workers, the proportion of rapid epinephrine decreasers was significantly higher after than before a vacation period, which had improved the workers' physical and psychological well-being.[125]

Another example of conditions associated with slow unwinding was provided in a recent study of stress and coping patterns of female clerks in an insurance company.[126] It was hypothesized that an additional overtime load would call for increases in adaptive efforts, the effects of which would not be confined to the extra work hours, but would also materialize during and after regular workdays. The results supported this hypothesis, in that catecholamine excretion was significantly increased throughout the overtime period, both during the day and in the evening. As hypothesized, there was a pronounced elevation of epinephrine output in the evenings, although these had been spent under nonwork conditions at home.[111,127] This was accompanied by a markedly elevated heart rate as well as feelings of irritability and fatigue. In sum, these results demonstrate how the effects of work overload may spread to leisure hours.

Impact of Mass-Production Technology

Over the past century work has been fragmented, changing from the completion of a well-defined job activity with a distinct and recognized end-product, into one of numerous narrow and highly specified subunits with little apparent relation to the end-product. The growing size of factory units has tended to result in a long chain of command between management and the individual workers, accentuating remoteness between the two groups. The worker becomes remote also from the consumer, since rapid elaborations for marketing, distribution, and selling interpose many steps between producer and consumer.[128]

Mass production normally involves not just a pronounced fragmentation of the work process but also a decrease in worker control of the work process, partly because work organization, work content, and pace are determined by the machine system, partly as a result of the detailed preplanning that is necessary in such systems. This usually results in monotony, social isolation, lack of freedom, and time pressure, with possible long-term effects on health and well-being.

Mass production, moreover, favors the introduction of piece wages. In addition, heavy investment in machinery, alone or combined with shorter hours of work, has increased the proportion of people working in shifts.

Another effect of the emphasis on mass production, and eventually on automation, is that large industrial concerns have grown at the expense of medium-sized and small enterprises.

Work on the assembly line, organized on the principle of the "moving belt," is characterized by the machine system's rigorous control over the worker. The job is understimulating in the sense that individual operations are often extremely simple. In addition, there are no options for variety in either pace or content, and the opportunities for social interaction are often minimal. At the same time the work contains elements of overload, such as rapid pacing, coercion, and demands for sustained attention. The worker has no control over pace, and his body posture and motility are narrowly restricted.

In their now classic study, Walker and Guest[129] showed how assembly-line work, with its mechanical element and rigidly fragmented tasks, was accompanied by discontent, stress, and alienation among workers. Similar results have been reported by other investigators.[130,131] Studies that focus on the task structure and its variations within similar technologies underscore that the restrictions imposed on the workers as to exercising skill and control may lead to alienation and loss of motivation.[132,133]

By integrating concepts and methods from psychophysiology and social psychology it has been possible to link both job dissatisfaction and physiologic stress responses to specific job characteristics.[111,134]

In a study of sawmill workers,[113] interest focused on a group classified as high-risk workers on the basis of the extremely constricted nature of their job. The psychoneuroendocrine stress responses of this group were compared with those of a control group of workers from the same mill, whose job was not as constricted physically or mentally. The results showed that catecholamine excretion during work was significantly higher in the high-risk group than in the controls. Furthermore, the time course was strikingly different in the two groups, catecholamine excretion decreasing toward the end of the workday in the control group, but increasing in the high-risk group. Interview data showed that inability to relax after work was a serious complaint in the latter group. Moreover, absenteeism and frequency of psychosomatic symptoms were very high in this group. The data suggest that the high stress level in the acute work situation and the symptoms of failing health had a common origin in the repetitious, coercive nature of the job. Thus, correlational analysis showed consistent relations between psychoneuroendocrine response patterns and job characteristics in terms of monotony, constraint, and lack of personal control.[113] These relationships were examined further by comparing subgroups of workers who differed with regard to specific job characteristics as rated by experts. The results indicated that stress, as reflected in catecholamine excretion, was highest when the job was highly repetitious, when the worker had to maintain the same posture throughout working hours, and when the work pace was controlled by the machine system. Thus, lack of control again stands out as the critical factor. The modifying influence of controllability on psychoneuroendocrine stress responses has also been demonstrated in laboratory studies of human subjects by Frankenhaeuser and her coworkers.[135–139]

A related issue is the relation between stress and a remuneration system involving some type of piecework.[140] The common factor in piecework systems is that payment is based on performance.

There may be a fixed relation between pay and units produced or the rate of pay may be pegged higher and higher with increased volume of production. For example, the hourly increment of pay may be 1.33% of each 1% increase in output. At low output the differences are small and scarcely apparent to the worker, but at high output they provide a powerful stimulus to the worker to step up production.

It is generally agreed that piece wages strengthen motivation and are thereby one of the most important incentives to boost productivity. It is often claimed that piece wages are a necessary prerequisite of good performance, yielding higher earnings for workers and lower costs for management.[108] Yet little is known about the psychological and physiologic effects of this remuneration system. It is, for example, conceivable that excessively strong motivation on a regular basis could lead to undue strain, which might be harmful to health and well-being.

The desire or necessity to earn more can for a time induce an individual to work harder than is good for him and to ignore mental and physical warnings, such as a feeling of tiredness, nervous troubles, and functional disturbances in various organs or organ systems. Another possible effect is that the employee, bent on raising his output and earnings, breaks safety regulations, thereby increasing risk of occupational disease and of accidents to himself and others (eg, lorry drivers on piece rates).[140]

Elderly or handicapped employees working in groups with

collective piece rates are liable to come under social pressure from their fellow workers and employees. On the other hand, when piece rates are individualized, workers may be disinclined to help each other.

A large state-owned mining company experienced a steep decline in severe accidents (cases requiring more than 90 days sick leave), and a smaller decline in medium severe cases (seven to 90 days of sick leave) after fixed salaries were substituted for piecework pay. The loss in productivity was only 10% in the mining operation and there was no decline in productivity in the more automated plants.[141,142]

In Swedish forest industries, 1-year follow-up studies of the introduction of fixed wages in logging show a reduction in severe accidents. In one case the total number of accidents decreased by 10%, while days lost through accidents were reduced by 50%.[143] Both companies report productivity losses of about 10% to 15% but at the same time increased product quality.[144]

The above observations from epidemiologic studies are supported by experimental investigations.[108,145] Healthy female office clerks were studied under conditions very similar to those involved in their everyday work. Highly progressive piece wages were introduced on the first and third days of the study, and were found to result in significant increases in productivity but also in feelings of rush, fatigue, and physical discomfort, in elevated epinephrine and norepinephrine excretion and in urine flow.

In summary, these and related findings point to piece rates being a factor with several negative aspects from the viewpoint of stress, health, well-being, and safety. Above all, piece rates seem to induce an intensified working rhythm, a strong tendency to take risks, and competition between individuals or teams.[146] Obviously piece rates also may lead to increased productivity, but possibly at a cost carried by the worker and society at large.

Impact of Highly Automated
Work Processes

An important question is whether occupational health and well-being will be improved, while the strain on the workers diminishes, by a transition to automated production systems where the repetitive, manual elements are taken over by machines, and the workers are left with mainly supervisory controlling functions. This kind of work is generally rather skilled, it is not regulated in detail, and the worker is free to move about.[129,133]

Accordingly, the introduction of automation is generally considered to be a positive step, partly because it eliminates many of the disadvantages of the mass-production technique. However, this holds true mainly for those stages of automation where the operator is indeed assisted by the computer and maintains some control over its services. If, however, operator skills and knowledge are gradually taken over by the computer—a likely development if decision-making is left to economists and technologists—a new impoverishment of work may result, with reintroduction of monotony, social isolation, and lack of control. Only when the computer is introduced as an advanced tool to assist and help the worker, will the outcome be beneficial. With the striving toward maximum automation, man may again become the tool of his own tools!

For these reasons the work conditions of control-room operators in large-scale plants deserve special attention.[111,147,148] Monitoring a process calls for acute attention and readiness to act throughout a monotonous term of duty, a requirement that does not match the brain's need for a moderately varied flow of stimuli in order to maintain optimal alertness. It is well documented that the ability to detect critical signals declines rapidly, even during the first half-hour, in a monotonous environment.[149] In addition, the fact that the process operators work in shifts means that they may have to perform their attention-demanding task when out of phase with their biological rhythm, ie, when epinephrine secretion is low and ability to concentrate reduced.[108,150,151] To this must be added the strain inherent in the awareness that temporary inattention and even an intrinsically slight error could have extensive economic and other disastrous consequences.[107,111,122] These are the demands put on eg, the process operator in the control room of nuclear power plants.[151,152]

Other critical aspects of process control are associated with very special demands on mental skill. The operators are concerned with symbols, abstract signals on instrument arrays, and are not in touch with the actual product of their work. Research is needed to analyze the psychological implications of such requirements.

High technical skill is required of process operators, yet they spend most of their time in monotonous monitoring. How, in the long run, will these highly skilled operators cope with conditions that utilize their skill during only a fraction of their work hours?

While we have referred mainly to industrial automation, similar questions arise in connection with highly computerized administrative work. Office workers may spend up to 90% of their day at a computer terminal. As long as the computer system functions adequately, the work runs very smoothly. But the moment the computer breaks down, the worker is helpless and is forced to remain in a state of passive expectation for an unpredictable period of time, turned into a bottleneck, holding up the flow of work.[111] These mechanical breakdowns occur irregularly, but tend to be frequent and are always unpredictable. They constitute a source of stress, reflected at both the psychological and physiologic level.[153] Here, as in the case of highly automated industrial production systems, stress research is needed to provide knowledge that can aid in guiding technological developments to suit human needs and abilities. The aim should be to achieve a level of automation that is optimal for ascertaining a meaningful work content and adequate demands on workers' skill. Optimum automation thus defined is not likely to be the same as maximum readily available automation.

Reciprocal Impact of Occupational and Other Social Structures and Processes

Social structures outside work can influence health and well-being in the work setting as well as outside it. For example, although inadequate housing is in no way the only factor making it difficult for a shift worker to sleep during the day, attention to housing factors may facilitate getting and staying asleep. Another example of structural factors outside work whose effects need to be studied and their modification evaluated is the long distance between workplace and home as well as inadequate public transport that forces the worker to spend much time in commuting, often under crowded or otherwise unpleasant conditions that are difficult to control. Exposure to such conditions has been demonstrated to result in increased epinephrine excretion.[154,155]

Insufficient or inadequate day care for preschool children may add very considerably to the stress experienced by working parents and their children. But availability of day care is just part of the problem. Its quality is also important, as was shown in a crossover study, in which an increase in the number of nurses per child group was introduced into the psychosocial environment of 100 3-year-old children in ten day care nurseries. A longitudinal and interdisciplinary evaluation of the effects[156] demonstrated a decrease in child stress in terms of epinephrine excretion and behavioral deviations, as well as in nurse stress, in terms of a sharp decline in absenteeism, with possible secondary effects on the situation and health of the children's parents.

The design of industrial and office buildings can make it difficult or impossible for handicapped workers to fulfill their duties.

To immigrant workers, a cultural shock may be added to the normal occupational stressors. Ability to cope may be decreased further by insufficient knowledge of the language spoken at work.

Briefly, conditions outside work can influence occupational stress, health and well-being. Similarly, occupational stress can result in a spill-over into the workers' existence outside work. Studies have shown that narrow and socially isolated jobs create passivity or social helplessness. Workers who never participate in planning or decision-making, who rarely cooperate with or talk to other people during the workday, who are doing the same old routine day in and day out, probably learn to act in basically the same way in situations outside work as well. They belong to what has been called the "politically poor," expressed in low political and trade union activity, and thus to the groups who are worst equipped to deal with their own problems. One set of studies shows that when the exercise of discretion in work is curtailed by spatial, temporal, or technical restrictions built into the work process, the individual's ability to develop active relations during his spare time will diminish. Persons whose jobs entail serious constraints with respect to autonomy and social interaction at work take far less part in organized and goal-oriented activities outside work that require planning and cooperation with others.[120,157,158]

A representative survey of the Swedish male labor force carried out in 1968 has shown that workers doing psychologically unrewarding work take much less part in various organized leisure activities than persons who do not have such jobs. This finding is especially true for cultural, political, and trade union activities of a kind which require active participation and communication with others. Their leisure activities center around the nuclear family, sports and outdoor life, and the television.

This study was repeated 6 years later, in 1974. It was found that those whose jobs had changed during the period in the direction of a richer job content and greater say on the job showed an increased participation outside the job in voluntary associations, study work, and trade union and political activities. In contrast, those whose jobs had become more narrow and confined through computers or other forms of rationalization took less part in such activities outside the job in 1974 than in 1968.[119]

Stressful Aspects of Shift Work

Cyclical changes are an important property of all organic life. A special example of this rhythmicity are circadian rhythms, or those that occur in a 24-hour cycle. Many physiologic and psychological functions have been shown to exhibit circadian rhythms. The peaks and valleys of such rhythms usually correspond with potential demand. Thus, systems that respond to the environment are most active during waking hours. At least until recently, these circadian rhythms have been well adapted to environmental demands, favoring a variety of life- and species-preserving activities during the day and sleep during night.[159,160] But increasing demands for services and introduction of extremely expensive and complex modern technology have created social structures that require greater human occupational activity throughout the 24-hour day.

Such circumstances have led to creation of work shifts, in which people work at times other than during the usual daylight hours, eg, during late afternoon and evening or throughout the night. As a result, some individuals must work when they are out of synchrony with the usual circadian rhythms. These difficulties may be compounded greatly if employees are compelled to rotate shifts, so that they work during the days part of the time and during evenings or nights other times. These problems have been the focus of a series of interdisciplinary investigations utilizing experimental and epidemiologic approaches.[160]

In summary, these studies and a critical review of the scientific literature justify several conclusions.[161-163] First, physical, mental, and social problems and complaints increase with the introduction of night shifts and decrease when night shifts are eliminated. Major concerns are sleep, digestion, and possibly also cardiovascular problems. Problems of health and well-being and social problems tend to coincide in the same individuals. When workers are rotating through three shifts, complaints are usually most pronounced for those on the night shift. Second, increased absenteeism is found in elderly shift workers, even though there is no overall increase in absenteeism in shift workers in comparison to dayworkers. This suggests that adverse consequences of shift work may be cummulative or more pronounced in older workers. Third, workers on permanent night shift exhibit a better biological adaptation than do those on rotating shifts; compared to dayworkers, their circadian rhythms are reversed, indicating that they are prepared for high levels of activity during the night. Such adaptation does not appear to occur for individuals who are on rotating shifts, regardless of the length of exposure.

CHAPTER 7

STRESSFUL ASPECTS OF SHIFT WORK

KRISTINA ORTH-GOMÉR

Cyclical changes are an important property of all organic life. Special examples of this rhythmicity are diurnal rhythms, biological functions which fluctuate during a 24-hour cycle and circadian rhythms with a 24-hour periodicity. Among such inherent rhythms are sleep and wakefulness, swings of body temperature, cortisol and growth hormone secretion, digestive and other activities. The peaks and valleys usually correspond with normal day-night energy demands. Until recent centuries, these rhythms have been well adapted to life- and species-preserving activities during the day and sleep during the night.[107,159] But, modern demands for production and the need for allnight services have required occupations to continue throughout the 24 hours of the day. Some people have had to be assigned to work shifts at times other than during the day, usually during late afternoon and evening or throughout the night. Therefore, during shift work their bodies are forced to change their normal diurnal rhythms. When the bodily rhythms no longer coincide with environmental demands, they must become adapted to a new time cycle which is a slow process. Some of the biological rhythms are less adaptable to a new time cycle than others. Further complications may result from conflicts arising from the worker's social environment where family adjustments and other social adaptations have to be made.

Available evidence suggests that the use of two shifts during the 24 hours is better tolerated than three shifts. However, even that arrangement can produce some strains on the worker, such as problems with access to breakfast and public transportation for employees on the morning shift. Difficulties that can be associated with the afternoon shift include decreased interactions with preschool and school children, relatives and friends, as well as limited opportunity to participate in cultural, political, and social activities.[161] When there are three shifts to cover the entire 24-hour period, major disturbances may be unavoidable. Of particular importance are the social obstacles that those working on the night shift face in trying to secure a relatively long continuous period of time in which to make up for a sleep deficit. These difficulties may be compounded greatly if employees are compelled to rotate shifts, so that they work during the days part of the time and during the evenings or nights at other times.

The difficult time adjustments for the eight-hour shift workers are well known, but less familiar are the abilities of individuals to adjust their physiologic and social functions to the eight-hour time shifts around the clock. Some of these problems have been the focus of a series of interdisciplinary investigations utilizing experimental and epidemiologic approaches.[162,163]

LABORATORY EXPERIMENTS

An interesting study has examined temporal variations of some important physiologic functions in the absence of the normal time cues. More than 100 healthy volunteers of both sexes were required to work continuously for three days and three nights.[160] Despite strict standardization and equalization of environmental stimuli, most diurnal and circadian rhythms persisted throughout the vigil. During the night, there were pronounced decreases in epinephrine excretion, body temperature, and performance, and increases in fatigue ratings and melatonin excretion.[150,160,164-166]

INTERDISCIPLINARY-OBSERVATIONAL STUDIES

A logical second step in studying the potential health effects of shift work was to look for persisting biological rhythms in a real-life situation, where environmental demands conflicted with them. Physiologic, psychological, chronobiological, and social reactions were investigated in response to a requirement for 3 weeks of nightwork for habitual daytime workers.[167] During the test period, the endocrine system started to adapt to the environmental demands by shifting its diurnal cycle, but took longer than 1 week for complete adaptation. In fact, even after 3 weeks of nightwork, the original rhythm cycles had either flattened or persisted for most subjects. These disturbed biological rhythms were associated with difficulties in sleeping and abdominal discomfort. In addition, a switch from habitual daywork to three weeks of nightwork was accompanied by increased evidence of physiologic stress and of social problems of the workers and their families.

REAL-LIFE EXPERIMENTS

Observations of adverse effects were confirmed in an epidemiologic study of the well-being of a large group of shift workers.[168-170] In the area chosen there were no other jobs available near where the workers lived, thus minimizing the chances of self-selection to or away from shift work. Health questionnaires showed higher frequencies of sleep, mood, digestive, and social disturbances among shift workers than among dayworkers. Complaints about lack of well-being were most common during the night shift. In a natural experiment within this setting, two experimental groups were switched to two-shift work, either night- or daywork. A 2-year follow-up demonstrated that the change to such two-shift work schedules was accompanied by improved physical, mental, and social well-being.[111] In contrast, a comparable control group who remained on its habitual three-shift work schedule showed no such improvements.

In shift work, the individual must endeavor to adapt both biologically and psychosocially to this interference in normal daily rhythms. In an experiment to improve the conditions of shift work, carried out at the Laboratory for Clinical Stress Research and the National Institute for Psychosocial Factors and Health, Stockholm, the attempt was made to make adaptation to shift work easier.[171,172] The study surveyed work conditions and health indicators for 747 uniformed policemen working shifts, and included an experiment to improve work conditions on the basis of the results of the survey. Fifty-two percent of the policemen were dissatisfied with their working hours, and even more stated that they would be willing to forego extra pay for inconvenient working hours in exchange for a better shift work schedule.

The experiment to improve work conditions was based on the following consideration: It was found that the biological daily rhythms, the circadian rhythms, are approximately 25 hours long in most persons and thus do not fully coincide with the 24 hours of the astronomical day. This circumstance makes it easier for most people to lengthen the day somewhat, ie, to go to bed a little later every day rather than vice versa.

An examination of the policemen's rotating shift work schedule revealed that the schedule forced the policemen to go to bed a few hours earlier each new day in the workweek. Thus, they had to adapt to a successive shortening of the day. The intervention was simple: the rotation was changed to a clockwise from a counterclockwise rotation (Figure 7-1).

In this way the work schedule was accommodated better to the natural daily rhythms. At the same time, the officers also obtained a longer time to rest between work shifts.

72

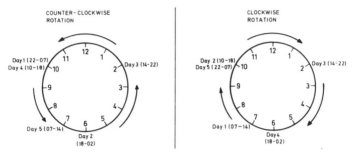

Figure 7-1 Counterclockwise (left) and clockwise (right) shift rotation schedules used in an experiment to improve shift work schedules of uniformed policemen.

The new schedule was tested in an experimental crossover study in which two groups of policemen worked on each of the two schedules, the new and the old, for 4 weeks, after which they exchanged schedules with one another. The effects on both subjective assessments and physiologic parameters were studied. Sleep was improved and fatigue reduced.

Serum triglycerides, glucose, and uric acid were significantly lower during clockwise as compared to counterclockwise rotation, but the differences disappeared after termination of the schedules. Systolic blood pressure, which was only measured after schedules, also decreased with the clockwise rotation.

Habits of tobacco and snuff consumption remained unchanged throughout the two schedules. Although it was not possible to keep dietary habits under strict control, it seems reasonable to assume that they did not differ between schedules to any greater extent than did smoking habits. However, if any policemen used eating as a means to cope with stress and fatigue, an improved work schedule may have improved dietary habits and thus accounted for changes of, eg, lipids and glucose.

As anticipated in the study design, work load estimated by the number of reported police actions did not differ between the two schedules. Subjective ratings of work strain also were similar.

The general sense of well-being, however, improved with the clockwise rotation. This was perhaps best demonstrated in the change of sleeping habits. Sleep at night after daywork was reported to be longer and better with the clockwise rotation than with the counterclockwise rotation. The effect was more prominent during than after termination of schedules. Although the number of hours worked were the same on both schedules, the resting periods between work shifts were prolonged from approximately 12 to 20 hours on the clockwise rotation. This may have accounted for part of the beneficial effects on sleep. As a result of the prolonged rest between shifts, weekends after rotations were shortened with the clockwise rotation. This disadvantage may partly explain why satisfaction with the new schedule was not unanimous.

Irregular Working Hours

Approximately one third of the working population in Sweden must work inconvenient hours.[173] Many of these (about 10% of all those employed) have their work hours earlier or later in the day, which means a smaller divergence from ordinary work hours than in regular shift work.

Conventional shift work, with three shifts (one week of day shift, one week of evening shift, and one week of night shift) is the lot of about 5% of all employed persons in Sweden. Roster work, which means that working hours vary from one period to another on a rotating schedule, befalls about 8% of working people. A total of 10% of all employees have regular recurring nightwork.

A large proportion of persons working inconvenient hours are employed in the manufacturing industries. Most of these work in two or three shifts. Nursing personnel, police, post and telecommunications, and transport employees and other public service employees usually perform roster work.

Several recent cross-sectional studies of widely separate population groups indicate a high risk factor level for cardio-vascular disease among shift workers. In a study from Tromsø in northern Norway, 6595 men aged from 20 to 49 years were investigated with regard to risk factors for cardiovascular dis-ease as well as certain social and work-related variables. Nightworkers or shift workers proved to have higher serum cholesterol levels and to smoke more than day workers. Serum triglycerides and systolic and diastolic blood pressure were also somewhat higher than among dayworkers, but the dif-ferences were not statistically significant.[174]

In our study, making shifts rotate clockwise rather than counterclockwise caused some risk factors for cardiovascular disease to be favorably influenced (Figure 7-2). Systolic blood

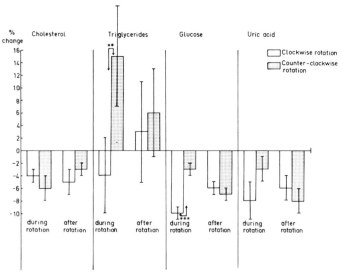

Figure 7-2 Some blood chemistry values compared in shift workers during and after clockwise and counterclockwise shift rotation.

pressure decreased, and blood lipid levels (triglycerides) and blood glucose levels were lower during the clockwise rotation than during the counterclockwise rotation. On the other hand, tobacco consumption did not change over the time of the study.

It is not clear how the high risk factor level for cardio-vascular disease in shift workers is to be accounted for. One might hypothesize that if, for a long period, blood pressure and blood lipids are not permitted to fall during the night as they normally do, then permanently high levels for both may gradually be established. In any case, the interpretation of the preliminary data presented here must await the results of the longitudinal investigations being carried out in Sweden.

CHAPTER 8

CHARACTERISTICS OF EMPLOYMENT THAT MODIFY THE RISK OF CORONARY HEART DISEASE

TÖRES THEORELL

Our purpose in this report is to provide a general survey of what we know about psychosocial factors at work in cardiovascular disease, with reference to the complicated interplay between the individual and the environment with which no simplistic unilinear approach can possibly deal adequately.

WORK CONDITIONS

Most people spend about a third of the day at work. Work is woven into our other activities as well. We often choose to be together with our workmates in our private lives too, and the content of our jobs influences how we shape our leisure time. Several studies[175,176] have demonstrated a correlation between the stimulation provided in a job and how active a person is in his leisure time. It is therefore difficult to isolate the effects of work as such on cardiovascular disease. Nonetheless it is of interest to attempt to characterize occupational groups that have an uncommonly high or uncommonly low risk of myocardial infarction.

It is now well established that the risk of cardiovascular disease is greater for men in low status occupations than in occupations with high status. We have also seen that the differences between social groups are only partly responsible for differences in traditional risk factors.[177–181]

If we accept that myocardial infarction is today more common among less well-educated persons,[182] three kinds of questions come to mind:

1. Those which demonstrate that the same genetic factors are behind low income and proneness to cardiovascular disease.

2. Those which claim that poor living habits of relevance to cardiovascular disease follow special groups; the lower the social group the more risk factors. This would mean that people in low status occupations also smoke more, are more overweight, and eat more harmful fats than others[183] *without this having any correlation with the content of their work.*

3. Those which demonstrate that the job situation as such has perceptible effects on physical risk behavior (smoking, eating habits) as well as on neuroendocrine mechanisms of importance to cardiovascular disease (see below).

Explanations falling into group 1 do not seem very likely since a social career is decided upon long before the pathologic mechanisms leading to heart disease have had a chance to produce symptoms perceptible to the individual. Explanations falling into groups 2 and 3 are often difficult to separate. They are probably woven together into a complex system. A work environment that demands steady concentration but gives no natural stimulation or possibility of controlling the work pace may cause a worker to begin to smoke more for stimulation,[184] and also to establish a psychological reaction pattern. In this way the direct effects of the work environment give rise to a "social inheritance" that creates a changed set of initial conditions for the children.

STUDIES OF PSYCHOSOCIAL FACTORS AT WORK AND THE RISK OF MYOCARDIAL INFARCTION

The first studies published in this area were retrospective, ie, persons who had had myocardial infarction were interviewed and asked about their work conditions before they became ill. An approach of this kind can result in mistaken assessments of the presumed correlations, in part because only persons who have survived myocardial infarction can be interviewed. What, indeed, is the case becomes a relevant question inasmuch as prospective studies (ie, studies in which healthy persons are interviewed and then followed up to see which of them become ill) in general have shown weaker correlations between psychosocial work conditions and the risk of myocardial infarction than have retrospective studies. Is a person heading for a myocardial infarction more inclined to deny the problem before than after the infarction (if he survives)? Might perhaps a person exaggerate his problems afterwards to have an explanation for his infarction? In the first case, prospective studies would underestimate the correlation, and in the second case retrospective studies would overestimate it. We do not know which interpretation is correct. Some studies indicate that persons who have high blood pressure but do not know it neither complain of physical symptoms nor go on the sick list more than others. As soon as they learn that they have high blood pressure, on the other hand, the reverse is the case; complaints and absenteeism increase beyond the norm.[185] This would seem to indicate that retrospective "exaggeration" is a problem. On the other hand, prospective studies have shown that individuals who died from myocardial infarction during a ten-year follow-up period were "clearly more optimistic and adopted a more denying attitude with regard to future problems and difficulties" than persons who survived their infarction.[186] This indicates that "prospective underestimation" can also be a problem in the most serious forms of cardiovascular disease.

The retrospective studies of the relationship between psychosocial factors at work and cardiovascular disease may be divided roughly into those who stress overwork and those who stress maladjustment.

Overwork

In his large studies of Bell Telephone Company employees, Hinkle[86] showed that an individual who worked full time and attended evening college during the same period ran a high risk of dying from myocardial infarction. But the author also pointed out that many forms of increased workload were not associated with high risk. Promotion was such a factor. Shekelle et al,[187] in 1979, in a study of civil servants in Chicago, found that a yes answer to the simple question "Do you work under severe pressure?" was associated with a high risk of myocardial infarction during a ten-year follow-up period even when smoking habits, blood lipids, and blood pressure were taken into account as possible factors. Kittel et al[188] studied two banking firms in Belgium, one seminationalized and one private, and showed a higher incidence of high blood pressure and a higher incidence of myocardial infarction in the private firm. Differences in body weight or smoking habits were unable to account for these differences; the job situation was therefore analyzed and found to be quite different in the two cases. In the private firm significant changes had been introduced at the beginning of the observation period which during the years in question had led to a fierce work pace with hard competition for higher positions, while in the other firm work was more evenly paced.[188]

A study of construction workers in Stockholm[189] covered all male 41- to 61-year-old members of the construction workers' union in the greater Stockholm area, who were asked to fill in a psychosocial questionnaire. Some of the questions referred to the work situation in the year just past and were called "psychosocial job strain." Changes in job responsibility, a subjective sense of an unjust burden of responsibility on the job, change of occupation, conflicts with superiors and workmates, as well as the threat of unemployment were all included. Those who answered yes to at least one of these ions were deemed to be under psychosocial strain.

he frequency of reported psychosocial job strain was r among those who suffered myocardial infarction, espe- among those who previously had exhibited no signs of disease (Table 8-1), than among the others. On the other , no correlation could be demonstrated if the analysis was icted to those who died from myocardial infarction.

t was also interesting that the group of construction ers who had worked with the heaviest loads, namely con- e workers, had the highest risk of myocardial infarction. crete workers over the age of 50 with psychosocial work in had an especially high risk of myocardial infarc- .[189] The interpretation of these findings is a complicated

ible 8-1
bserved and Expected (Age-Adjusted)
roportion of at Least One "Yes"
esponse Within the Group of Questions
n "Psychosocial Work Load Last Year"
n the Building Construction Worker
Study (N=5187)

	All Cases of Myocardial Infarction (n=51)	Cases "Without Previous Symptoms" (n=31)
Median age	55	53
Observed rate of psychosocial work load (%)	37.3	48.4
Expected rate (%)	22.7	24.5
Ratio observed/expected	1.64	1.98
z value for comparison	2.49	3.09
P value	.01	.01

matter. The older concrete workers found it difficult to keep up the fast work pace with much heavy lifting. As a rule their wages were based upon group piecework, so that many of them may have experienced considerable pressure from their workmates when they were unable to do their share to keep up earnings. This may have set off psychosocial processes which in turn helped in some cases to hasten the advent of infarction.

These are hypothetical explanations which are difficult to demonstrate. Our purpose in describing them in such detail is to underscore that aging, physical strain, mental strain, and wage structure may be interwoven into a complicated pattern. Accepting that physical and mental overstrain may have contributed to an infarction, the following measures come to mind for reducing the risk for these groups: (a) Change the system for setting wage rates (which, in fact, was, in part, done since the studies were carried out); (b) Reduce the physical demands, especially for the oldest workers (which has also been done in some measure).

Maladjustment

In recent years, research in industrial psychology has called attention to the fact that *strain* in the form of hectic work pace, overtime, and role conflicts may differ in its effects depending on the situation in which the demands are made. Differences may arise because of individual factors (and factors having to do with an individual's general living situation without any bearing or particular relation to work) and because of differences in the organization of work.

The first group of studies done in this area were centered on the individual, eg, whether discontent with the job situation was more common among persons with cardiovascular symptoms than among others. Retrospective studies demonstrated such a correlation,[190-192] but prospective studies did not.[193]

"Discontent" is, of course, a vague term. The vaguer the questions asked, the more ambiguous the answers. More specific approaches have been used. Flodérus[194] did a prospective study in which she showed that twins who themselves recognized that they were unable to unwind after work ran a greater risk of angina pectoris than did others over a four-year follow-up period. Subjects who felt that they had too great responsibility or inadequate education for their job did not have a higher incidence of angina pectoris during the follow-up period but on the other hand did in general have a higher mortality. The trends were the same for monozygotic and dizygotic twins, which indicates that these associations are more environmentally related than genetic. In these results, which were based on questions concerning how the subjects perceived their job adjustment, it was found that different psychosocial job factors were associated with angina pectoris and mortality respectively during the follow-up period, which adds even more weight to the importance of keeping different manifestations of cardiovascular disease separate when these factors are studied.

The next group of studies was centered on the "fit" between the individual and his job situation; in the American and English literature this is called the person-environment fit. Comprehensive studies have demonstrated that the risk factors smoking, high blood pressure, and high blood lipids were more common among individuals whose expectations of their work environment did not accord with their job situations.[195,196] A number of studies on the type A pattern in relation to the work environment may also be said to belong to this group. Chesney et al[197] demonstrated, for example, that a work situation that was perceived as difficult to control may be associated with high blood pressure in persons with pronounced type A patterns, ie, persons who are highly competitive and in a continual rush. The same environment need not be associated with high blood pressure in persons lacking a type A pattern. This fits in well with the results of experimental studies that have shown that persons with a pronounced type A pattern respond with an especially sharp rise in blood pressure in situations characterized by a rush for time and the lack of means of control.[198]

Demands and Decision Latitude

The last group of studies concentrated wholly on the external conditions of work. Some experimental research has shown that a locked-in job situation with hectic pace (eg, on a production line conveyor) increased the secretion of adrenal hormones (cortisol, epinephrine, norepinephrine) more than other work,[199-201] while other epidemiologic research has concentrated on influence, stimulation, and margin for decision-making on the job. Since high blood pressure is one of the most important risk factors for cardiovascular disease, research on job structure and blood pressure is important. The published epidemiologic studies on self-reported work environment and blood pressure show either no correlation or fewer reported adjustment problems in the ill group than in the healthy group.[202] Whether this reflects the true conditions or just a tendency in persons with asymptomatic high blood pressure to underreport problems is not known. If one uses a "standardized" average evaluation of the situation in different occupational groups, the problem of individual underreporting and overreporting can be avoided. Such a study is described by Karasek et al,[203] in which sociological means were constructed for every occupational group with regard to demands and margin for decision-making on the job on the basis of work environment interviews in the years 1969, 1972, and 1977 with representative groups of working American men in over 200 occupations. Later, two other sets of survey data each comprising 2000 randomly chosen working American men — the Health Examination Survey (HES) 1960–1962 and the Health and Nutrition Examination Survey (HANES) 1971–1974 were used.

In these studies, data on occupational code (the same as in the treatment of occupational groups), age, education, smoking habits (HANES), cholesterol (HES), and systolic and diastolic blood pressure were available. A multiple regression analysis was done. In this procedure, the significance of every conceivable explanatory variable is weighed against all the other explanatory variables with regard to predicting an individual's blood pressure. Systolic and diastolic blood pressures were analyzed separately. Standard values for demands and margin for decision-making in a person's occupation, along with the person's age, education, smoking habits, and cholesterol levels, were used as explanatory variables.

The analysis showed that a low margin for decision-making in three of the four analyses (systolic in both groups, diastolic in one group) had a statistically significant correlation with blood pressure.

In a recent study of myocardial infarction we used a Swedish occupational classification system based on interviews with 3876 Swedish men working in 118 different occupations.[204] The "standard values" we obtained for the occupational groups have since been used to analyze data on 334 cases of myocardial infarction, ie, all men living in the catchment areas for Huddinge and Södertalje Hospitals aged between 40 and 65 years who survived or died from a myocardial infarction during the years 1974 to 1976 and for whom an occupational code was available in the population and housing census. These were compared with 882 men of the same age who had not suffered infarction and who lived in the same region. The analyses showed that monotony and shift work were the only psychosocial work variables showing a significant correlation with the risk of myocardial infarction. The term "monotonous work" is simply a reference to the fact that a high proportion of men in the occupational group had answered yes to the question, "Is your work monotonous?" Shift work is discussed in another section.

Occupations with many heavy smokers and a high proportion of persons who had no more than the mandatory schooling also ran a high risk of myocardial infarction. The obvious question is then: can the correlation between monotony and high risk of infarction be explained by the fact that many persons in high-risk occupations also happen to be heavy smokers or have a low level of education? We, therefore, also analyzed the conceivable confounding effect which smoking habits, education, and certain physical stress factors in different occupational groups may have on this correlation. It was found that the correlation between monotony and myocardial infarction remained regardless of whether groups with few or many smokers were analyzed. On the other hand, the correlation could be partly explained statistically by the fact that persons in monotonous occupations often had a low level of education and many physical stress factors. Groups with many poorly educated persons with much heavy lifting thus overlapped partly with those in which many persons reported monotonous work and partly with groups that ran a high risk of myocardial infarction.

Long work hours, a hectic pace, and risk of unemployment and accident showed no correlation with the risk of infarction in the same analysis. In the Swedish infarction analyses as well, it seems as if a low margin for decision-making is perhaps more important than demands as regards the risk of cardiovascular disease.

More recent studies of a limited margin for decision-making as a risk factor thus indicate that this may be a risk factor for cardiovascular disease, although the mechanisms behind this correlation remain unclear.

Karasek et al[205] have put forth the hypothesis that it is perhaps demands in combination with inadequate stimulation and margin for decision-making which are important for the development of heart disease.[205] Experimental stress research has shown that short-term reactions, as, eg, an increase

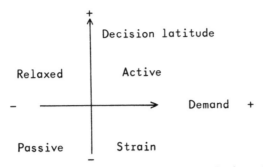

Figure 8-1 Karasek's two-dimensional job model.

in catecholamine secretion and a rise in blood pressure under pressure of time are impaired if at the same time the means of control are inadequate.[206] A study of persons working with data terminals in an office showed, eg, a clear rise in blood pressure in correlation with computer breakdowns.[207]

However, it has been difficult to carry out epidemiologic studies on human beings to determine effects of a more long-term kind on morbidity. Karasek[208] has formulated a hypothesis on these correlations. A job situation can be described in two dimensions: demands and margin for decision-making (which often are correlated with stimulation) (Figure 8-1).

A "strain" job entails many demands, often a rush for time or role conflicts,[199] for example, and at the same time a poor margin for decision-making. Moving along the diagonal from relaxed to strain in the diagram, physiologic reactions of the catabolic kind should, according to the theory, become increasingly pronounced. These are reactions with continuous physiologic activity, with no opportunity to replenish and restore that which, indeed, is always being used up and depleted in the body. Catabolic stress reactions, known to us from physiologic research, are, for example, secretion of the hormones norepinephrine, epinephrine, and cortisol, and in the cardiovascular system, high blood pressure, increased pulse rate, and heightened myocardial electrical excitability (which can give rise to irregular heart activity).

An "active" job entails many demands but also has a large margin for decision-making and considerable stimulation. This means that a person working at a hard job with much pressure of time is permitted to decide himself when to take a rest; he may, for instance, choose to shift his work to the evening hours or to the weekend. In addition, mental stimulation at work means physiologic stimulation, in that anabolic functions are activated. Such anabolic reactions are, for example, an increase in secretion of the hormones testosterone, estrogen, and insulin. These hormones stimulate the formation of new cells and enable the body more easily to withstand the catabolic processes which in a stressful situation may break down proteins or deprive the myocardium of "useful salts," eg, potassium and magnesium.[209] Pauses in a job under pressure of time can also play a major role in ensuring that overactivation never reaches extreme levels.

A "passive" job entails rather few demands and a reduced margin for decision-making, and relatively little stimulation. The theory tells us that as we move along the diagonal from passive to active a worker's ability to cope with stressful situations on the job increases.

In the Swedish studies[210,211] with interviews of 3876 Swedish men working in their occupations, we divided 118 professions into two groups: (1) the 50% with the most and the 50% with the fewest persons, respectively, reporting their work to be hectic; and (2) the 50% with the most and fewest persons, respectively, reporting that they had no control over the work pace. With this classification we can determine which major occupational groups fall into the different work pace quadrants of the diagram. Thus among occupational groups with strain work we find drivers, slaughterhouse workers, crane operators, and waiters. In the "relaxed" group we find university teachers, ministers, bank accountants, and precision instrument makers.

In the active groups we find journalists, firm managers, and tailors, and finally in the passive group we find concrete workers, plumbers, shop mechanics, watchmen, and military men. In the American studies[203] coweighted variables were constructed indicating demands and margin for decision-making. The occupational groups in the different quadrants of the diagram were still largely coincident with those in the Swedish study. The specific examples of occupational groups must be taken with some reservations. It must be kept in mind that an individual's situation may diverge considerably from the pattern for the whole group, and that the work situation in the different occupations is changing continuously.

If the theory is correct, it should be the individuals in occupational groups doing strain work who run a high risk of cardiovascular disease. This was first tested in the American study[203,212] in which investigations of randomly chosen men in the HES 1960–1962 and HANES 1971–1974 were able to draw on the findings of clinical examinations showing who had suffered a myocardial infarction. The results demonstrated that the prevalence of infarction was highest in occupational groups doing strain work. The correlation existed for all the age groups in the HANES but was somewhat less clear in the HES.

We also made use of the Swedish prospective study in Huddinge and Södertalje to shed light on this question.[213] Individuals in the occupational groups doing strain work according to the Swedish classification were compared with the other individuals. Table 8-2 shows the results of this analysis in the form of a comparison of age-corrected relative risks of myocardial infarction in which variables having to do with demands, namely, a great threat of unemployment, long work hours, shift work, piecework, a hectic pace, and a high accident risk, are combined with variables having to do with a low margin for decision-making and low stimulation, and with physical stress factors. The effects from the combination differ depending on the demand variables in the combination. For

Table 8-2
Age-Standardized Relative Risk of Myocardial Infarction for Persons (40–64 Years Old) Exposed at the Same Time to One Variable in the Group "Demands and Insecurity," and to One of the Variables in the Groups "Control and Possibilities for Development" or "Physical Demands"

	Major Threat of Unemployment	Long Working Hours	Shift Work	Piece Work	Hectic Work†	High Accident Risk
Monotony	1.3	0.9	1.3*	1.1	1.1	1.0
No private visits	1.2	1.1	1.4*	1.2	1.3	1.2
Little influence on work space	1.2	1.2	1.4*	1.1	1.4*	1.2
No contacts	1.1	1.0	1.2	1.1	1.2	1.1
No chance to learn new things	1.2	1.3	1.4*	1.0	1.5*	1.1
Sweating	1.1	1.2	1.4*	1.1	1.4*	1.1
Physical monotony	1.2	1.2	1.3*	1.1	1.3*	1.1
Heavy lifting	1.2	1.2	1.4*	1.1	1.4*	1.1
Noise	1.0	1.2	1.4*	1.0	1.2	1.0
Vibrations	1.1	1.1	1.3*	1.0	1.4*	1.0

*Significant to 5% level.
†Data from Alfredsson et al.[213]

the variables "large threat of unemployment," "shift work," "piecework," and "accident risk" there were no consistent trends, i.e, combination with low margin for decision-making, low stimulation, and physical stress factors yielded no real difference in risk. On the other hand, for "hectic work" and, to some extent, excessively long work hours, a definite pattern was visible which is especially distinct if one looks at the risks linked with a hectic work pace (which is not in itself associated with a high risk) in combination with the monotony variables. The psychosocial variables also showed a stronger correlation with relative risk in the age groups below 55 years. For the combination "hectic work pace" and "lack of control over work pace" the relative risk for myocardial infarct under age 55 years was 2.0, while for "hectic work pace" and "no possibility to learn new things" it was 2.3. One interpretation of this is that those who have a high risk leave occupations with a strain work situation when they approach the age of 55 years and so the correlation thereafter becomes less distinct. The monotony variables all show a correlation with one another and with low level of education, while "hectic work" and "long work hours" are wholly uncorrelated. The occupations with a high proportion of individuals reporting "hectic work" have even fewer individuals than expected reporting that they do not have more than the mandatory schooling, that they have no opportunities to speak with their workmates, that they have no major possibilities for learning new things, that they perspire every day, or that they are exposed continuously to deafening noise. These findings mean that occupation groups in which many report a hectic work pace for the most part have more stimulation and fewer physical stress factors than others. The observation that occupations with both a hectic work pace and monotony have a high risk of myocardial infarction becomes perhaps especially interesting in this light.

Relation to traditional risk factors The next question is whether the correlation between a hectic work pace and lack of control, on the one hand, and risk of myocardial infarction on the other, can be accounted for or is mediated by smoking habits or other relevant factors. According to the findings of analyses carried out so far, the correlation between strain work and risk of myocardial infarction cannot be accounted for by the frequency of heavy lifting, level of education, percentage of immigrants, or percentage of smokers in a given occupation.[213]

A study of registries of five Swedish counties seems to verify the importance of a combination of "hectic/no possibility to learn new things." The occupations of 640,000 men were identified in 1975. All hospitalized cases of myocardial infarction were identified in 1976. The same type of classification system was again applied, and occupations with reported combination of hectic/few possibilities to learn new things had more cases of myocardial infarction than expected even when several social variables, part-time work, number of cigarette smokers, and amount of heavy lifting had been taken into account. Once again the association was stronger for men below the age of 55 years than for the total age spectrum. Very similar patterns were observed for women.

In a Swedish follow-up study[214] of working men in the standard of living registry, 22 cases of death from myocardial infarction or cerebral stroke (embolism, thrombosis, or brain hemorrhage) occurred between 1968 and 1974. Each of these was compared with three men who did not die and who at the start of the follow-up period were comparable with respect to age, smoking habits, symptoms of cardiovascular disease, and education. The comparison was made to test the hypothesis that those men who in the interview had reported that their job was both hectic and physically stressful (high demand) and also both monotonous and requiring no education (low margin for decision-making) were overrepresented among the 22 cases of death. The correlation was statistically significant for the demand variable. For the combination demand/margin for decision-making, the sample was too small to test the hypothesis, but the results spoke in favor, especially inasmuch as a follow-up study of the development of cardiovascular symptoms carried out at the same time confirmed the hypothesis that the development of symptoms can be predicted by the combination high demand/low margin for decision-making.[205]

To sum up, our studies have so far indicated that a combination of high demands and low margin for decision-making is a significant risk factor for myocardial infarction. The mechanisms underlying this correlation are unknown, but a rise in blood pressure may perhaps be contributory.

Blood Pressure Changes in the Work Setting

Previous observations by our group and by Karasek and coworkers[210,215] have indicated that the risk of myocardial infarction is elevated in occupations in which the pace is hectic and the opportunity for initiative and decision-making on the part of the worker is small. Our data also indicate that occupations with a small decision latitude have a larger proportion of smokers than other occupations. This correlation, however, does not explain all of the association between type of occupation and risk of myocardial infarction.[216] Another possible mechanism may be that repeated marked elevations of blood pressure during the workday may increase the risk of myocardial infarction.

Using modern devices for recording arterial blood pressure, several researchers have reported large fluctuations during daily activities, particularly among persons with borderline hypertension.[217-219] We therefore set out to ascertain whether certain types of work contribute to such blood pressure fluctuations. The investigation was made on young healthy subjects and unmedicated subjects with largely asymptomatic early-stage hypertension.

Material The groups studied were selected from the military draft board. Potential participants were selected from those who participated in the medical examinations for the military service—all 18-year-old men in the area—in the years 1969 to 1974. Blood pressure was recorded during two consecutive days according to standardized procedures. The pressure recorded under the most basal conditions was utilized. Those with at least 146 mmHg systolic and 90 mmHg diastolic formed one group. Comparisons were made with a group in the middle of the distribution (126 to 130 mmHg systolic) and also from the lower part of the distribution (100 to 106 mmHg systolic). They were labeled hypertensive, normotensive, and hypotensive, respectively. In the hypertensive sample, 81 subjects had been examined medically during the period 1969 to 1974. When the present study was performed approximately 10 years after the original examination (during the period 1981 to 1982) four of these originally selected subjects had moved to other countries or parts of Sweden whereas two subjects had died. Thus 75 subjects remained for the study. In the two other groups, 35 normotensive and 34 hypotensive subjects were randomly selected. Four subjects in the normotensive and three in the hypotensive group had moved outside the greater Stockholm area. Thus 75, 31, and 31 subjects remained for the present follow-up study in the three original samples respectively. Of these 56 (75%), 27 (87%), and 23 (70%) subjects in the hyper-, normo- and hypotensive groups, respectively, participated in the follow-up. To make the numbers more comparable the normo- and hypotensive subjects were treated as one group. Seven refused recordings of blood pressure during the workday although they participated in the other parts of the follow-up examination. Two of them were unemployed at the time of examination. Table 8-3 displays the group means for systolic blood pressure. The lowest average is recorded outside work for the normo-hypotensive group in occupations

Table 8-3
Group Means ± SD Based on Average Blood Pressures at Age 30 Years (106 Subjects)

	Normo-Hypotensive at Age 18 y – "Nonstrain Occupations" Now	Normo-Hypotensive at Age 18 y – "Strain Occupations" Now	Hypertensive at Age 18 y – "Nonstrain Occupations" Now	Hypertensive at Age 18 y – "Strain Occupations" Now
Systolic blood pressure outside work	121.5 ± 8.8	124.2 ± 8.5	136.1 ± 8.3	135.3 ± 14.3
Systolic blood pressure at work	125.4 ± 8.1	126.2 ± 8.9	144.4 ± 12.4	152.6 ± 24.8

labeled as "nonstrain occupations" (BP 121.5 mmHg). The highest average systolic blood pressure (156.2 mmHg) is recorded at work for those subjects who had high blood pressure at the age of 18 years and are working in "strain occupations" today.

Results Table 8-4 shows the results of the corresponding analysis of variance. It is seen that subjects who had high blood pressure at the age of 18 years were the most likely to have high blood pressure 10 to 15 years later. Strain occupations appeared to have effect only on blood pressure at work. Blood pressure was significantly higher at work than outside work, particularly in the originally hypertensive strain occupation category.

The corresponding results for diastolic blood pressure also indicate that the lowest blood pressure on average is recorded outside work among subjects who were hypo- or normotensive at the age of 18 and are working in nonstrain occupations today (BP 74.8 mmHg), while the highest pressure is recorded

Table 8-4
Analysis of Variance for Systolic Blood Pressure

One-Way Analysis	F	P
Initial group at age 18 y (hyper-/normo-/hypotensive)	44.4	.001
Type of work (nonstrain/strain occupation)	1.0	.31
Condition (at work/outside work)	40.6	.001
Two-Way Analysis		
Initial Group/type of work	0.1	.72
Condition/initial group	15.5	.001
Condition/type of work	2.0	.16
Three-Way Analysis		
Condition/initial group/type of work	4.7	.03

at work in the initially hypertensive subjects now working in strain occupations (BP 87.1 mmHg).

Conclusions The study concluded that subjects who exhibited an elevated blood pressure at the age of 18 had greater elevations of systolic blood pressure from the outside-work to the at-work condition when they were followed up at the approximate age of 30, particularly those who were working in strain occupations. This partly supports the hypothesis proposed by Karasek et al[205] who had stated that work conditions are particularly strainful psychophysiologically if they imply a combination of psychological demands and constraints on action, in this case hectic work with little opportunity to control the pace. The observations further suggest that only a part of the population is affected, namely those who already have a propensity to hypertension.

It has been pointed out by other authors that temporary blood pressure elevations, if marked and repeated frequently, may have significance for the development of heart muscle hypertrophy and deterioration in heart muscle function.[220,221] The findings in the present study indicate the potential benefit of decreasing extreme combinations of high demand and low decision latitude in certain jobs.

CHAPTER 9

CONTRIBUTIONS OF THE EMPLOYEE'S PERSONALITY AND BEHAVIOR TO OCCUPATIONAL STRESS

CLINTON G. WEIMAN

Stress-related bodily disturbances seen in the company medical department cover almost all organs and organ systems. Skin disorders associated with pruritis, such as urticaria and eczema, are common as are headache, backache, stiffness, and pains in and around the joints of the extremities that stem from muscle tension. There is an equally rich profusion of gastrointestinal (GI) complaints, some of them without associated anatomical lesions and others less prevalent such as peptic ulcer and ulcerative colitis, which are classified as organic diseases. The array of disturbances, including accidents, is contributed to in a major way by an individual's own peculiar problems encountered in coping with life at work, at home, and elsewhere.

Susceptibility to incapacity from such stress-related disturbances is found among 20% to 30% of workers and executives. Available evidence suggests that susceptibility to incapacity is inherent in the person and his way of looking at and responding to the people and events in his environment. There are many stresses to be dealt with in the workplace, including the ever-advancing waves of new technologies, the spectre of job insecurity and economic instability, and the often complex personal problems related to the corporate hierarchy itself.

Vulnerability to this combination seems especially characteristic of those determined to climb the corporate ladder, despite what they perceive in themselves as handicaps of background and education. One such patient was a 46-year-old corporate vice president who described his difficulties in an interview with the medical director as follows:

ANXIETY STATE

Patient: Most recently I've experienced more tenseness and more apprehension than I have ever experienced before. Primarily within the last year, I have experienced occasional shortness of breath and of being irritable, being keyed up, being just overall tense and ready to explode.

I put a lot of long hours into a lot of very pressure-filled assignments; I've experienced tension headaches in the back of my head, right-hand corner of the back of my head. I've had a lot of tension headaches. I've been hospitalized for the full battery of tests because I was very dizzy at work and I was nauseous and I felt like I was going to pass out. I spent four days in the hospital and the tests revealed nothing physically wrong with me at the time I was in the hospital other than the high blood pressure I had when I was admitted. Subsequently I experienced other situations at work where I have been dizzy or felt nauseous. I feel nauseous just about every morning before I come to work when I know it's going to be a difficult day, that is, a tension-building day. I get the dry heaves quite frequently in the morning. I feel on edge quite a bit.

I feel like I have to get everything done—everything has to be done in one day.

Doctor: Did you ever go to your supervisor about this?

Patient: The first time I went to my supervisor was today.

Doctor: Why didn't you go before?

Patient: I was very concerned that if I did go to management with this, that it would affect my career. I am a vice president now and I was an assistant vice president when these symptoms started. I was afraid I would be called a quitter or I would be demoted. You know I couldn't handle that. They would say, "Let's get somebody good." I was afraid to admit that.

Doctor: Tell me something about your background, how you got to your position in the bank.

Patient: I graduated from high school. I was at another bank for 5 years. Then I came here in 1969 as a clerk. I worked my way up to vice president by going to college at night for 10 years. Between all the pressure I had to put up with I was able to get married and have three children and I have a nice home.

Doctor: What have you done to reduce the tension?

Patient: Well I try to acknowledge it may be self-induced. It might be me that is the cause of my own tension. I've tried to relax. I've been to a biofeedback session with a doctor to see if I could relax more. While I was with the doctor I did relax and everything seemed fine, but when I was working it didn't help.

Commentary: This 46-year-old man was a predictable victim of his own early experience and psychological make-up. His parents were first generation immigrants and they raised him in a large urban community. While in high school he worked nights and weekends to assist the family with routine household expenses. It took him 10 years to qualify for a college degree. While attending college at night he was slowly rising in the organization of the bank to positions of increased responsibility. He also found time to marry and purchase a small home.

With each step up the corporate ladder, he assumed more responsibility, worked longer hours and spent less and less time at home.

About 1 year prior to the onset of his anxiety and tension syndrome he was promoted to vice president. It appeared that this last promotion was the one that did him in. Somehow it seemed he was on a work roller coaster and did not know how to stop it.

All of the work stressors he experienced were quite likely his self-imposed unrealistic goals combined with fear and self-doubt. This is evidenced by his delay in bringing the work overload to the attention of his supervisor until the day he came to the medical department. The fear manifested by his belief that he would be demoted or be replaced by someone "good" was unfounded. He also lacked the courage to bring the situation to the attention of his supervisor. When the supervisor discussed the matter with the medical department there was no mention of inadequate performance.

The physiologic expressions of this worker's reaction to the stressors were predetermined by his early life experience and career path. His life-long work pattern was characterized by long hours, heavy self-imposed responsibilities, and an inordinate fear that his superiors might think he was a complainer. Even a passing thought of complaining would evoke a guilt feeling which in turn would probably make him work still harder and longer.

MYOCARDIAL INFARCTION

Among the more catastrophic illnesses that seem to occur at times of special stress are myocardial infarctions. An alert company physician can often spot the worker who is likely to suffer a heart attack. Characteristically a smoker, he may have a family history of heart attacks, and be overweight. From a personality standpoint such susceptible workers may be fearful of failure and reluctant to share responsibility or delegate it. Many of them find it is difficult to work for superiors and tend to be argumentative. Once a decision goes against them they tend to brood over it, rather than move on to new challenges. Although they submerge themselves in work, they seem not to gain satisfaction from it.

The following case of a 53-year-old executive illustrates some of the elements in the background and personality of the employee and the special features of his work situation that may have combined to precipitate a myocardial infarction. The resolution of the problem may have contributed to 3 years of well-being and freedom from complaints.

Jack W., a 53-year-old white male executive, had worked for his company since he graduated from college some 30 years ago. Jack was brought up in a banking family so he had a good idea about where he wanted to go in the company. For a long time he had a secret yearning for a particular job in the organization. The occupant of that job was due to retire in the near future so Jack's anxiety level was increasing as he saw the possibility of getting that job.

Jack had always been a self-controlled, self-disciplined person and, aside from his immediate family, no one knew he aspired to this particular job. Along came the corporate announcement indicating someone else had been selected for the job Jack wanted so much. A month later Jack suffered a myocardial infarction. He apparently made an uneventful recovery and returned to his job. His superior asked him to report to the medical department for clearance to return to work, but instead he requested his private doctor to send the medical department a copy of his ECG. In this way he avoided the visit to the company doctor as well as corporate documentation of his heart attack. The belief that the company medical department can influence an executive's career, however, is usually and should always be unfounded.

A few years later, the officer who had been assigned the coveted job was transferred to another area, so again the job became a possibility for Jack. He was offered and accepted the position. Almost at once there was an evident change in his behavior.

Shortly thereafter at a corporate function, I overheard a conversation between Jack and an associate. Jack told his friend he was enjoying his new job, the one he had always wanted in the corporation.

Jack's long yearning for this job for many years, followed by the disappointment of not getting it, may have been a significant contributing factor to his heart attack.

While one can never identify with certainty the precipitating factors of a myocardial infarction, it is likely that Jack's temperament and his way of looking at life were of some etiologic significance. Jack was a dedicated, hard-working intensely loyal executive who was rigidly controlled and not prone to share his innermost feelings with his associates or superiors. When he failed to get what he wanted most he became depressed, sad, and maybe even angry. Unfortunately, this is not an isolated occurrence in corporate America.

HYPERTENSION

Another common disorder, essential hypertension, was found in 20% of 5000 employees in one company. The typical hypertensive patient encountered in industry appeared to be outwardly calm, ambitious, but not overly confident. He or she was often resentful of authority but was firmly determined not to fail. Discussion with such patients revealed a well-concealed fear of criticism or rejection. They characteristically denied being overworked lest they be labeled as complainers.

SMOKING AND OVEREATING

Smoking and poor dietary habits are aspects of individual personality and behavior problems, which may act synergistically with other factors to bring about adverse medical consequences. A compulsive need to smoke approaches alcoholism in its close association with disease and premature death. Although in one company during a 20-year period of study fewer than half of the employees were smokers, nevertheless over the years 75% to 80% of those who died while still employed were cigarette smokers. The close association with fatality was consistent whether the cause of death was heart disease, cancer, homicide, or automobile accidents. It seems obvious that in physical fitness programs currently popular with corporate management, a special emphasis on smoking behavior is needed.

Although in recent years the number of male cigarette smokers has gradually decreased, as women move into highly competitive positions in industry, there has been an increase in the number of women who sustain myocardial infarcts. Whether these changes are related to the decreasing prevalence of myocardial infarction among men and its increase among women has not been determined.

Since cigarette smoking is associated with increased mortality and morbidity for all major illnesses it serves as a potent catalyst to increase the effects of occupational stress. Cigarette smokers are absent from work more than nonsmokers. When an employee is absent someone else may have to take on additional duties. As a result, the cigarette smoker puts an additional burden on his or her fellow employees. The cigarette smoker also puts an added burden on his fellow worker by using health care benefits to a greater extent than the nonsmoker.

If any addiction rivals cigarette smoking's tenacious hold on its victims, that addiction is overeating with its consequent

obesity. Like cigarette smoking, overeating may be accentuated during periods of emotional tension, thereby acting in
concert with occupational and other stresses. The psychological consequences of overeating are often cumulative as obesity
diminishes self-esteem. The failure of repeated diet regimens
to produce sustained weight loss may contribute to emotional
depression. Like cigarette smoking, obesity is well known to
predispose to cardiovascular and other diseases.

CONCLUSIONS

Stress-related disorders, not only anxiety states and so-
called functional disturbances of the gut and other tissues but
some potentially fatal diseases such as myocardial infarction,
appear to depend to a substantial degree on the individual
characteristics and the behavior of the person affected. Behaviors such as smoking lend themselves to quantification.
Other less quantifiable behaviors that reflect aspects of a person's temperament and the way he views and deals with adversity may exert equal or even greater influence. Whether
or not to attempt in advance of employment to identify inherent vulnerabilities and proclivities toward stress-related
diseases poses a difficult dilemma for the employer. Attention
to individual characteristics which may lead to disability may,
however, be appropriate after employment.[2]

In any case, it is ironic that the legislative mandates to
the Occupational Safety and Health Administration (OSHA)
failed to direct attention to the common stress-related disorders of employees but deal instead with less widespread hazards of toxic chemical exposure, etc. Similarly, the research
program of the National Institute of Environmental Health
Sciences is focused almost exclusively on the tangible hazards
of the workplace. Fortunately, the medical departments of corporations have shown increasing interest and concern with
stress-related illnesses as described elsewhere in this volume.

CHAPTER **10**

ALCOHOL AND OTHER MOOD-CHANGING DRUGS

THOMAS C. FLEMING

THE CHICKEN OR THE EGG?

Stress is frequently cast in the role of a universal culprit spawning all sorts of unpleasant conditions from simple nervous tension to medically labeled disorders such as hypertension, peptic ulcer, coronary heart disease, psychologic "burnout," anxiety reaction, and last—but certainly not least—alcoholism and other forms of substance abuse.

In a recent survey,[222] just under half of a group of alcoholics and their families attributed the problem of alcohol abuse to stress, and primarily stress arising from interpersonal conflicts.

The obverse side of this cause-and-effect relationship is probably a more realistic proposition—namely, that stress, in its varied forms, is more likely a *result* rather than a *cause* of alcoholism.

DEFINITIONS

Alcoholism: In these discussions, the term alcoholism is used in its broadest sense to define a disease associated with the chronic, repetitive use of alcohol or any mood- or mind-changing drug in such a way that it interferes with any aspect of a person's life. These aspects include health, job performance, community status, and relationships with family, friends, fellow citizens, and working associates. Thus alcoholism will be used interchangeably with such terms as chemical dependency, substance abuse, and addictive disorders.

Stress: Webster's dictionary suggests that stress can be regarded as a state of "bodily or mental tension resulting from factors that tend to alter an existent equilibrium."[223] The theme of this chapter is that alcohol, when abused, is an etiologic factor that can alter the existent equilibrium in the lives of all persons involved with a substance abuser; and the resultant disruption in equilibrium is manifest as a state of stress.

RISK OF ADDICTION

Can we predict when the use of alcohol as a social or gastronomic grace note—or as an occasional antidote to transient anxiety—may turn on the user and become a harbinger of future stress? Alex Comfort has answered this query in a thoughtful fashion.[224] He reminds us that while the use of an addicting drug such as alcohol may be contained for a period of time, "a benign coexistence cannot be guaranteed to the individual . . . . vulnerability is unpredictable until the damage is done." Despite a growing recognition that certain prognostic patterns may warn of future addictive problems, it is impractical, as of today, to screen on a broad scale for highrisk persons in our society.

THE SCOPE OF THE PROBLEM

Few stress-inducing factors can match alcoholism in universality and societal penetration. Alcohol easily outranks all highly publicized pollutants as an environmental hazard. In public health terms, alcoholism deserves to be classed as an illness of epidemic proportions.

Few would debate that ill health causes stress to both the sufferers and their immediate families. According to a recent report in the *Annals of Internal Medicine*,[225] alcoholism is America's third largest health problem. The US Office of Technology Assessment estimates[226] that between 10 and 15 million Americans are either alcoholics or alcohol abusers with up to 35 million persons directly affected. These sources also implicate alcohol in one half of deaths by motor vehicle accidents and fires.[225,226] It is a major factor in divorce and a cause of 40% of domestic problems brought to family court.[226] Alcohol abuse is involved in about 67% of drownings and murders and 35% of suicides, while up to 33% of hospitalized adults have problems that are directly alcohol-related.[225] The economic cost in the United States is estimated to be as high as $120 billion annually.[226] Despite this, only about 15% of persons with alcohol-related problems receive treatment for their underlying addictive illness.[226]

In Britain in 1977, alcohol misuse resulted in £ 300–500 million in lost output irrespective of health and social-service costs.[227] Citing these statistics, an editor in *Lancet* remarked, "If the amount of alcohol-related diseases continues to rise we face a gloomy financial and social toll by the end of this century."[228]

In Russia, alcohol abuse has reached epidemic proportions. There, life expectancy for males is declining at an alarming rate—from 66.2 years in 1965 down to 61.9 years by 1984. Rampant alcoholism is by all accounts the main cause of this ominous trend.[229] Between 25% and 50% of the average Russian household's food budget goes for alcohol[230]; and in 1976 alone, 40,000 fatal cases of acute alcohol poisoning were reported.[230] It is difficult to contemplate this catalogue of human adversity without recognizing the enormous magnitude of the stress in all elements of society throughout the world which result from alcohol abuse, not to mention other chemical dependencies.

At any one time, it is estimated that drinking seriously interferes with the job performance of 6% to 10% of our work force.[231] A 1979 survey by the Opinion Research Corp,

Princeton, NJ, revealed that 18% of employees in middle and top management admitted concern over their own drinking habits.[231] In recent years, abuse of drugs other than alcohol has surfaced as a smaller, but increasingly troublesome element in the workplace. Total corporate losses in the United States have been placed at $77 billion[232]–$28 billion in productivity alone.[233] An alcohol- or drug-impaired worker making $18,000 a year may cost his or her employer upward of $50,000 to $75,000 annually in unplanned expenses.[234] Lists of such losses include a wide variety of items. Absenteeism runs anywhere from two- to fourfold to 16 times that found in comparable nonabuser employee groups.[235,236] Insurance benefits for accidents and sickness are usually about three times greater,[232] with additional losses incurred from sick leave and the overtime paid to coworkers covering for their chemically disabled colleagues. Losses from missed sales opportunities, consumer dissatisfaction, and damaged material expand the list, as do increased personnel turnover and the cost of replacement training. Less evident in dollars-and-cents accounting are the indirect costs attributable to impairment in concentration, judgment, and decision-making capabilities. Finally, there is the oft-ignored toll in human affairs manifest by family discord, divorce, abandonment, and child abuse. All these factors are as real as the price of labor, factory maintenance, taxes, or interest on debt. It is also worth noting that monies spent to cover substance abuse costs represent a total and irredeemable loss to the employer and the total economy.

THE PHARMACOLOGIC EFFECTS OF ALCOHOL

It is 5 PM, after a rough day at the office. The classic cry rings out: "Boy, do I need a drink!" In our culture, the normal day-to-day stress of work is regarded as a valid reason for self-medication with the socially accepted sedative drug, alcohol.

Here we may have the first element in an interesting neuropsychopharmacologic chain reaction.

Step 1: Stress (normal) ⟶ Alcohol use (normal)

But habitual repetition of this normal (?) drinking pattern may exceed the limits for that benign coexistence between user and substance mentioned earlier in this chapter. When this occurs, the stage is set for the second step in our sociobiochemical reaction. Drinking behavior now becomes an inducer of stress.

Step 2: Stress ⟶ Alcohol misuse ⟶ Stress

Here, stress becomes the sum of normal stress plus alcohol-induced stress. Our five o'clock script might now go: "The boss was pretty teed off when I dented his car in the parking lot coming back from lunch. Now I *really* need a drink!" Medically, what we are seeing is the very early outline in the clinical picture of a potentially protracted drug use and an associated insidious withdrawal syndrome that pleads for relief with more alcohol.

The diagrammatic progression of this self-catalyzing reaction to step 3 and beyond is predictable.

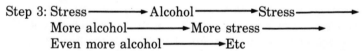

Step 3: Stress ⟶ Alcohol ⟶ Stress ⟶
More alcohol ⟶ More stress ⟶
Even more alcohol ⟶ Etc

Any attempt to interrupt this pathologic progression with increased intake of alcohol *or any other mood- or mind-changing drug* is to court failure and the ultimate disaster of serious addictive disease.

The malignant force driving this reaction to its inevitable, stressful and destructive conclusion is the persistent neuropsychopharmacologic effect of alcohol on the CNS.

Decades ago the Scottish entertainer Harry Lauder delighted audiences with his lyrical good news that "There's something in the bottle for the morning." This anticipated matutinal stress and its welcomed relief of the traditional "hair of the dog that bit you" is a homely, yet perceptive, example of the dual pharmacologic action of alcohol.

Anne Geller has observed: "Drugs in the sedative-hypnotic class [such as alcohol] have two particular effects: they depress the nervous system when the drug level is up, and they cause a rebound excitement of the nervous system when the drug level falls."[235] The higher centers of the cerebrum are affected first, while the equilibrium controls in the cerebellum are next to go, followed by those functions dependent on the spinal cord and life-sustaining medullary centers. Our interest is primarily in the effects of alcohol on the higher centers which determine what Stanley Gitlow describes as our "psychomotor activity level."[236] After taking a drink, the rapid rise of alcohol in the blood decreases psychomotor activity and gives the user a sense of relief from all those annoying, worrisome, uptight, and anxious feelings. This sedative phase only lasts about two hours. A second phase follows marked by an increase in psychomotor activity as the alcohol blood level begins to fall.

This second, longer-lasting, excitatory effect may have begun immediately after drinking, but it is overshadowed by the more dominant yet short-lived sedative effect.[236] Thus, with each dose of alcohol, the transient sedative "glow" is superseded by a more persistent agitation which may leave the drinker more tense than when he took the first drink. If he was uncomfortable then, think how he must feel now! But relief is still just another swallow away. This will be succeeded, unfortunately, by yet another rise in psychomotor activity as his alcohol level declines again. And so the cycle goes on until a stressful state of chronic agitation prevails.

If the cycle is abruptly interrupted, agitation will mount further with the withdrawal becoming manifest as alcoholic tremors (the shakes), convulsive seizures, hallucinations, and eventual delirium tremens. Attempts to stave off withdrawal by the chronic, repetitive use of alcohol can result in a less dramatic but more persistent form of misery, the protracted withdrawal syndrome. Both the sufferer and those around him may understandably perceive this syndrome as a state of chronic stress. But this state of stress is the *result,* not the *cause* of the disorder. And should this condition of unwellness continue and interfere significantly with any important aspect of the person's life, it is—by our definition—alcoholism. The abuse of other drugs leads to a comparable sequence of behavioral disturbances and symptomatology with characteristics distinct for each class of substances.

THE DRAMATIS PERSONAE

Thus far we have considered the cause-and-effect relationship between alcohol and other mood-altering substances and stress as it pertains to the individual employee. But the misuser of addictive substances does not perform in a one-man show. The alcoholic or drug abuser is never alone on stage. The roles played by a host of costars, supporting actors, bit players, and walk-ons are inexorably linked with that of the central character. And in the worst tradition of the theater, our leading man has also seen fit to cast himself as producer, playwright, set designer, and director. In all things he is indeed the center of distraction.

A perceptive psychiatrist was close to the mark when he labeled the active alcoholic "His Majesty the Baby," whose every giggle, whimper, and tantrum demands the attention of all around him.

In the terms of our present concern, the alcohol-induced stress in the central character affects all members of the company both on and off stage. So our dramatis personae must include the boss and the star's coworkers, as well as family and friends, and a chorus recruited from the audience representing the business and community world through which our drama moves.

The Boss

When the average boss attempts to control or manage the stress-related performance deficit of an alcoholic employee, it is usually "no contest."[234] Through years of practice, the alcoholic has perfected his or her litany of alibis and excuses under the heading "I'm under stress because (*fill in the blank*)." By the end of any number of "disciplinary" sessions, the boss will likely be convinced that such a poor and innocent victim of family and other troubles deserves to drink. Outflanked, the boss reverts to the familiar retreat of cover-up—enabling the alcoholic to go on being ill and spreading his or her stress-laden problems throughout the entire workplace.

When promises continue to be broken, job assignments bungled, and deadlines missed, the boss becomes angry and hurt, hurt that a trusted employee—and perhaps friend—has let him down. These negative feelings grow as the situation inevitably worsens, which only serves to increase the boss's underlying frustration, tension, and stress.[237] Incidentally, if it is the boss who suffers from substance abuse, the scene may change, but the scenario remains pretty much the same in relation to *his* superiors.

The Co-worker

The pattern of cover-up of drink-related behavior in a fellow worker is familiar to people in industry and needs little amplification. An encouraging trend which may foster more effective detection and subsequent corrective action is the growth of the quality circle concept on the industrial scene.[238] In this organizational and operational technique—originally developed by the Japanese—each small cadre or platoon of workers has responsibility for the quality of the group's output. In this work environment, the disruptive influence of an active substance abuser may not be welcomed or easily tolerated, and co-workers may be less hesitant to push the offender toward an appropriate company-sponsored employee assistance program. The characteristics of these programs are discussed below.

The Family and Significant Others

Alcohol-induced stress within the family circle is evident earlier and is generally even more disruptive than in the workplace. Here we find "enabling" in its most highly developed form. Enabling—a trait of many families, friends, employers, and coworkers of alcoholics—means minimizing or cushioning the destructive effects of the alcoholic's behavior. Such enabling is achieved by denying, covering up, lying, or making excuses for behavior, or by other protective gestures. There is, for example, the story of the master of the house who, suffering with a lethal hangover, requests his wife to pray for him. "Dear Lord," she implores, "please help my drunken husband." "Don't tell him I'm drunk," the sufferer insists, "tell him I've got the flu." Living with an alcoholic can make liars of the most upright of spouses.

This shattering of a significant other's value system can be a weighty stress indeed. And as the repeated misuse of alcohol induces the stress of a chronic illness on the abuser, so it takes an equal—if not greater—emotional and physical toll on the family and other concerned persons. Insurance statistics have shown that medical payments for the alcoholic's family are significantly higher than for noninvolved households. The overall cost to individuals, families, businesses, and the nation is incredibly high.

The Community

Just as alcohol and drugs can undermine individuals, families, and coworkers, so their abuse can stress those involved with the alcoholic from the larger segments of the community—customers offended by salesmen who smell of booze, litigants shortchanged by tipsy judges, bus riders terrorized by drunken fellow passengers, teenagers maimed by intoxicated teen-aged or adult drivers, sick persons ill-treated by alcohol-impaired physicians. Add the financial and human losses mentioned earlier and ask what price the community as a whole pays in alcohol- and drug-induced stress. The problem for most businesses and organizations is compounded by a widespread lack of knowledge about addictive illness and especially the disease of alcoholism. Substance abusers need first to be identified and then helped in an effective way.

DETECTION AND INTERVENTION

C.S. Lewis once wrote: "You cannot see things till you know roughly what they are."[239] In the same way, you can't perceive alcohol- and drug-induced stress unless you know what you are looking for.

Three features highlight the behavioral problems of the alcohol abuser: undependability, unreliability, and unpredictability. It may also be helpful to look for some of the following signs in addition to the obvious flushed face, red eyes, and alcohol-tinged breath:

1. The search for—or association with—drinking companions within or outside the workplace
2. A recital of elaborate excuses for erratic performance or behavior
3. A pattern of mood swings, eg, postlunch euphoria followed by midafternoon ill-humored lethargy
4. Tremor—often best revealed on examining handwriting with magnifying glass
5. A pervasive aura of aftershave, perfume, or mouthwash at unexpected times and places such as 3 PM conferences.
6. Frequent unscheduled absences from work area and visits to restroom with briefcase or large handbag

7. Repeated yet vaguely defined health problems and accidents

But above all, a high degree of awareness and suspicion should be cultivated. If there is a suspicion that the observed stress is alcohol- or drug-related, it is usually borne out.

In 1982, an article in the *New England Journal of Medicine* began with the statement that "Although ethanol [beverage alcohol] is widely used for its mood-altering effect, it is a toxic substance that directly or indirectly causes impairment of cellular function in every organ of the body."[240] Other mood- or mind-changing drugs may differ in the degree to which they alter the biochemistry of the brain and body tissues, but their stressful effects on individuals and their environment are no less dire.

For most managers and supervisors, "drugs" other than alcohol are something new in their workaday world. Alcohol, the most toxic of commonly used habituating substances, is at least a familiar and legal adversary. But just when the boss has become reasonably comfortable in confronting alcohol-related absenteeism in his top foreman, he catches the production manager sniffing cocaine from a hollowed-out ballpoint pen while his director of sales turns up as a polyabuser of an exotic mixture of jet-set goodies—and alcohol.

In all of these situations one is dealing with a chemically induced stress that significantly affects work performance through absenteeism, chronic lateness, or deteriorating relationships with other employees. Active therapeutic intervention is indicated as soon as the problem is clearly recognized and defined. Early intervention improves the chances for successful outcome. Unfortunately, some supervisors may fear that confrontation may be more painful than letting things go on as they are, with the vain hope that things may get better by themselves. The National Institute of Alcohol and Alcohol Abuse (NIAAA) has estimated that such procrastination can reduce the potential for recovery as much as fivefold.[234]

Prior to confronting the employee regarding problems related to substance abuse, the supervisor should be thoroughly familiar with personnel policy as well as services available through any existing employee assistant program (EAP). Evidence of declining work performance and unauthorized use of alcohol or drugs on the job should be documented in writing. The time, place, and list of persons who could be effectively involved in the intervention should be worked out ahead of time and the confrontation orchestrated so as to handle anticipated denials, alibis, and excuses proffered by the employee or potential enablers. In some communities skilled professional intervention specialists are available for consultation and guidance.

Specific treatment plans and appropriate referral channels should be established beforehand – going as far as to have the "suitcase packed." One should not hesitate to involve – either by initial participation or on standby – any concerned persons including well-briefed family members, close friends, coworkers, company health personnel, and clergy. The family physician can often be a valuable ally (alcoholism is a treatable disease).

An established working relationship with in- and outpatient detoxification, and hospital and rehabilitation facilities can be very helpful. Provision, through the personnel department, should also be made for sick leave and financial coverage of medical expenses as well as family needs.

It is also incumbent on the personnel department to (1) inform all employees of policy, procedures, and available assistance programs, (2) protect employees' interests on their return to the workplace, and (3) maintain confidentiality on both written and verbal levels. A national study conducted by the Association of Labor and Management Administration and Consultants on Alcoholism (ALMACA) revealed that 78% of salaried employees fear that their case data will not be kept confidential. They also expressed the wish for better indoctrination of upper management about alcoholism.[233]

Thomas J. Delancy, Jr., an executive director of ALMACA, emphasized that EAPs must have the support of top people in labor and management. Both groups should recognize their stake in improving employee health and thus productivity; this requires a commitment to programs on the part of both personnel officers and central labor councils.[233]

Many problems can and do arise in the operation of any intervention system. However, EAP activities have been a great help both to management and the individuals suffering from addictive disease. By 1980, EAPs were operative in over 5000 companies including about 60% of the *Fortune* 500.[234]*

CONCLUSION

The presumption of stress arising out of substance abuse may seem more theory than proven science. The results have not been systematically recorded in terms of changes in blood pressure, heart rates, hormone levels, or other quantitated physiologic or psychologic responses. Much of what has been said is based indirectly on estimates of economic and societal losses derived from observations of changes in the quality of human relations. Despite this, the concept of alcohol- and drug-related stress has a convincing reality in its own right. This reality was expressed eloquently in 1968 by Ruth Fox, a New York psychiatrist. What she wrote is derived as much from the spirit as from a scientifically trained intellect. Her conclusions are based on a lifetime career studying and treat-

---

*For more detailed information and guidance, interested readers may contact the Association of Labor-Management Administrators and Consultants on Alcoholism (ALMACA) 1800 N Kent Street, Arlington, VA 22209; or the Occupational Program Branch, National Institute on Alcohol Abuse and Alcoholism (NIAAA) 5600 Fishers Lane, Rockville, MD 20857. For an updated list of State and Territorial Occupational Program consultants, contact National Clearinghouse for Alcohol Information, PO Box 2345, Rockville, MD 20852.

ing sufferers from addictive diseases. She entitled her statement *Imagine Such a Disease.*[241] The cost and casualty figures of 1968 are puny compared to today's more compelling statistics, but the message remains as cogent as the day it was written. It serves well to summarize in human terms the impact of "alcohol as an etiologic factor in stress."

If some new and terrible disease was suddenly to strike us here in America, a disease of unknown cause probably due to noxious gas, or a poison in our soil, air or water, it would be treated as a national emergency with all our citizenry uniting as a man to fight it.

Let us suppose the disease to have so harmful an effect on the nervous system, that 5 million people in our country would go insane for a period lasting from a few hours to weeks or months, and recurring repeatedly over a period of from 15 to 30 years.

Let us further suppose that during these spells of insanity, acts of so destructive a nature would be committed that the material and spiritual lives of whole families would be in jeopardy with a resultant 25 millions persons cruelly affected. Work in business, industry, professions, and factories would be crippled, sabotaged or left undone; and each year more than $1\frac{1}{4}$ billion would need to be spent merely to patch up in some small way the effect of the disease on families whose breadwinners and mothers have been stricken.

Finally let us imagine this poison or disease to have the peculiar property of so altering a person's judgment, so brainwashing him, that he would be unable to see that he had become ill at all—actually so perverting and so distorting his view of life that he would wish with all his might to go on being ill.

The dread disease mentioned above is actually here, and it is ALCOHOLISM.[241]

CHAPTER 11

PROBLEMS OF AGING AND RETIREMENT

HELEN GOODELL

Everyone who lives long enough will eventually become enfeebled and so be unable to work. The burden of years is undeniable since in time the most vigorous person will slow down and the healthiest or most iron-willed will become less and less able to cope with the stringent demands of the workplace, no matter how leniently or compassionately applied, and with the hazards of getting to and from the job. Illnesses, moreover, are more disabling as homeostatic mechanisms, with age, become less effective. The rate at which the handicaps of aging appear, however, varies tremendously from person to person. Incapacity may be evident before 50 or may be staved off until after 90 years of age.[242]

The wide disparity in the time of onset of disability appears to be in part a function of genetic inheritance but other factors may also contribute to one's rate of decline or, conversely, to the lasting quality of an individual's vigor and initiative. Important among such determinants may be the social environment created by the values and customs of a family, a neighborhood, a region, or a cultural group in which an employee's attitudes and behavior were shaped.

The remarkable health and longevity of the Abkhasians of Georgia in the USSR was discussed in chapter 2. The salubrious social forces that prevail there have also been identified in other communities.[44] Roseto, a small town (population 1600) in eastern Pennsylvania, was also described in chapter 2. In Roseto the elderly enjoyed an important social role and exerted a significant influence in family and community affairs; at the same time they were cared for and catered to.[44] They presided over family conclaves in times of trouble and were frequently looked to for advice on family and community problems. Moreover, they had specific responsibilities in the household, including some degree of supervision of the children. Thus in Roseto the elderly played an important role in the life of the family and community. Instead of being shelved when their children became the principal financial providers, aging parents were in a sense, "promoted to the Supreme Court."[44]

Most Rosetans at the time of our original study in the early 1960s worked in the slate quarries of nearby Bangor and Pen Argyl, in local shirt or blouse factories, or in industrial firms in the Lehigh Valley about 25 miles away. The majority avoided retirement as long as possible and, if forced to retire because of company policy, continued working as helpers in local contracting firms or other businesses. The biography of one Rosetan, a blacksmith still at work at 83, was written by a neighbor against the perspective of the work ethic of that cohesive community.[44] His subject's motto was "work till I die," while pointing out that many senior citizens make the mistake of doing nothing when they retire. "After a long active life, they expect to suddenly stop all activity. When this happens, they become unhappy, bored and overwhelmed by a feeling that they are leading a useless existence. A sense of being useful is very important to retired people even if the work requires only one hour a day to complete."[243]

THE INSTITUTION OF RETIREMENT

The widespread practice of mandatory retirement grew out of the social security legislation enacted in 1935 during the New Deal era.[244] One of the aims of this legislation was to create more job vacancies by retiring older men and women. At that time age 65 seemed reasonable and life expectancy for men at that age was a little under 12 years. By 1967 life expectancy at age 65 had risen to 13 years. And with the research now going on to reduce mortality from cancer and cardiovascular conditions, presumably life expectancy will increase still further.

As more American people graduate to the older age bracket, vigorous objections to mandatory retirement are being heard. The pressure to allow people to stay at work beyond the conventional retirement age of 65 is being felt by state and national legislatures. Already in some situations the retirement age has been raised to 70, and the age limit for US government employees has been eliminated. Very few industries have followed the government's lead, however.

According to a study made by Harris and Associates for the National Council on the Aging, Inc, most older people in this country have the desire and potential to be productive, contributing members of society.[244] The case for optional retirement was forcefully presented by Paul Woodring in an article appearing in the *Saturday Review.*[245] In a speech delivered at the AMA Aging Conference in Boston, D.B. Allman said:

> At the dedication of the Leonard Davis School of Gerontology at the University of Southern California, retired United States Senator Sam Ervin spoke out against mandatory retirement. He said the retirement test should be: 'Whether people want to work and need to work.' If subject to retirement at age 65, Winston Churchill, British Prime Minister from 1940 to 1945 and from 1951 to 1955, would have been retired in 1939; Albert Schweitzer would have been shelved in 1940. Famed scientist Vladimir Ipatieff fled Russia, learned English at age 63, and then made major contributions to petroleum research during the next 22 years of his life. Such a list can be multiplied many times.[246]

Not only may mandatory retirement deprive society of the energies and talents of many capable and talented older workers, but on some individuals it may inflict an injustice, depriving them of the opportunity to work.

There are serious financial considerations as well. Contributions to social security are increasing for both employer and employee. At the same time social security income is sharply curtailed in the event of retirement before age 65. There are indications that the borderline age may even be raised, as the population of senior citizens increases and the size of the social security fund fails to keep pace.

DEMOGRAPHIC CONSIDERATIONS

During the present century the number of Americans aged 65 and over has increased from 3.1 million in 1900 to over 23 million in 1980. The proportionate increase of the elderly has been even greater. In 1900 4% of the population were 65 years of age or older; in 1980 the percentage had risen to 11%. The US Census Bureau recently reported that there are now more adults aged 65 and over than there are teenagers. And the trend toward an older population will only accelerate as the baby-boom generation reaches old age.[247-250]

"The consequences of this demographic shift are enormous, affecting everything from health care to job opportunities to fashion to pensions to advertising."[250] Advertising campaigns are already being tailored to attract consumers over 55 years old. Ten years ago admen were deaf to complaints about stereotypes of old people as sick, bothersome, or boring. Lydia Bragger, 80-year-old head of the Grey Panthers Media Watch, is having some success with her campaign against "ageism" as older people are beginning to be portrayed in advertisements as useful contributing members of society. The fact is that only 5% of the over-65 population in this country live in institutions, while the rest, more than 23,000,000, live and cope as active citizens and consumers. The old idea that intellectual decline is an inevitable consequence of aging has been pretty well exploded. The present view is that intellectual impairment is either the consequence of disease or possibly of disuse associated with social isolation and depression. The gravest disease of old age is Alzheimer's disease, formerly called senile or presenile dementia.[251] It affects less than 1% of the over-65 population but is under increasingly active investigation by medical scientists.

The harmful effects of isolation and the absence of social and intellectual stimulation in old age have been described in a monograph by Arnetz et al.[80] Perhaps, by staying socially involved and maintaining some intellectual interests, most people should be able to preserve their mental capabilities throughout old age.

As mentioned above, retirement from work is a development of recent times. In 1900 two thirds of American men aged 65 years and over were still working. By contrast, in 1980, only one fifth of those 65 and older still held jobs. Retirement with its various economic benefits and ultimately social security is largely the creation of the negotiating efforts of unions. The consequences have been salutary as well as stulifying. Retirement has made possible for some an escape from the drudgery of the daily grind. It has also created opportunities for younger workers wishing to move into already crowded job situations though agreements for optional early retirement after a designated number of years of work. The report of a special task force to the Secretary of Health, Education, and Welfare, published in 1973, reveals, not surprisingly that at one large industrial company, General Motors, 16% of the eligible unskilled workers, but only 9% of the skilled workers chose early retirement.[45] A 1965 Harris poll of retirees showed that more than half were dissatisfied with retirement, mainly because of financial strictures but also because of the loss of their work role.[252] The implications of these dissatisfactions for the health of the retirees have not been worked out, nor has it been established whether or not continued employment will contribute to lengthening the years of health and vigor. Perhaps it will for some but individual genetic endowment and sociologic factors such as the relatively exalted special role enjoyed by the elderly in such communities as Roseto may also contribute to sustained good health and the capacity to continue working.

SOCIAL CONSIDERATIONS

To the extent that a person can hold on to his job or land a new one, he tends to retain his identity as a worthwhile contributing member of the community. Mandatory retirement, even with the new federal standard of age 70, may no longer be a valid concept.

Faced with the prospect of retirement, however, even if eagerly looked forward to, a person must find or devise a new vehicle for his needs and aspirations. It need not always be a job. Apart from such special cases as Roseto, our society does not provide many older people continuing opportunities to contribute to society.

Increasing part-time opportunities for older workers is one way to address the issues of retirement, ease the burden on social security and pensions in general, and allow older workers the chance to continue to be productive. While still allowing retirees to enjoy more leisure time, part-time work gives employers the benefit of older workers' experience and skills, and will ease the coming labor shortages occasioned by low birth rates in the United States during the 1960s and early 1970s. It may even become necessary for employers to propose later retirement.

Although the problems of aging extend far beyond those of the workplace, they are inextricably intertwined with it. As business in the long run must adapt to trends in society, it should, if possible, anticipate those developments that will eventually require adaptation. Among relatively easily predictable circumstances that will increasingly affect the elderly is the reduced demand for unskilled and semiskilled labor because of increased reliance on automation. As a result, the surplus of unemployable unemployed, and retired persons will surely grow. Beyond this, prevailing retirement policies applying not only to unskilled but to skilled workers as well are swelling the ranks of the retired. Florida and other areas of the Sun Belt are thus filling up with those who have "earned" retirement, who spend money but produce no goods or services. The implications of enforced leisure for the health of these individuals has broader implications for the health of society at large.

When it is not feasible to prepare people to continue to earn money after retirement, it should be possible to prepare them for ways of seeking satisfaction and fulfillment through community involvement, continuing education, and volunteer work. It need not be reemphasized that a sense of personal significance and the satisfaction of achievement are powerful antidotes to the stresses of loneliness, boredom, and lack of purpose.

How the industrial community is to contribute to bringing about a more productive retirement experience has yet to be worked out. It is certain, however, that rational solutions are more likely to be arrived at if they are sought early, than if they are deferred until the shrill voices of organized pressure groups begin demanding a special kind of favoritism. Such coalitions have been heard from frequently in recent years. They have demanded and have often got one-sided concessions from a bewildered and poorly prepared public.

PREPARATION FOR RETIREMENT AND POLICY DEVELOPMENT

Since it is unlikely that the employment world will abandon the policy of retirement, it becomes appropriate for government, businesses, and private agencies to develop programs designed to help individuals to devise ways of continuing to exercise their potential after leaving the job. Already some American firms are preparing employees for useful retirement, and programs are also in existence in Great Britain, Australia, and Sweden. Action for Independent Maturity (AIM) a division of the American Association for Retired People (AARP), Washington, DC, has prepared a series of seminars with appropriate guidebooks to assist in preparation for retirement. They cover such subjects as housing, financial planning, legal affairs, health, attitude, and role adjustment. These programs and guidebooks are used by many companies, large and small. Some unions in the United States have preretirement meetings, lectures, and discussions aimed at making life for the retiree active, interesting, and economically stable. There are also federally sponsored senior citizens groups. The AARP accepts members 55 years old and over—actively employed, semiretired, or retired. The strength conferred by the very size of its membership, now more than 10 million, makes AARP an effective voice on behalf of all older Americans. Its educational and social service programs include preparation for retirement, crime prevention, defensive driving, health improvement, consumer aid, tax aid, and the Institute of Lifetime Learning, Washington, D.C. It also sponsors a program to utilize to the best advantage the capabilities of each of its members in a wide variety of volunteer jobs from teaching to foster grandparents to jobs in soup kitchens. Through its chapters scattered all over the country, AARP enables members to continue full, active lives in retirement by providing opportunities for significant community service.

As the proportion of the aged continues to increase in America it may become essential to a viable economy that the retired maintain some degree of productivity. Moreover, unless programs anticipating retirement are begun early, a person may find it almost impossible to adapt productively to the sudden change.

Since the decline of physical and mental capacities with age varies widely among different cultures and just as widely among individuals of a fairly homogeneous group, retirement-separation programs should match this variability with provisions for a wide disparity of physical and mental capability.

As an example of constructive retirement planning well in advance of actual retirement, Page has described the case of Herman S., composing room foreman in a printing shop since age 34:

Herm's employer knew the value of health maintenance and construction; seasoned experts like Herm, he knew, were not easily replaced. In the front office there was a complete file on Herm covering his aptitudes, his strong and weak points, his known likes and dislikes and his health. After Herm's 40th birthday, the boss saw to it that his file was taken out and brought up-to-date at fairly regular intervals. This involved medical evaluation by Herm's private doctor from time to time. The doctor knew what facets of Herm's health needed careful watching and what facets could safely be taken for granted.

In the course of time of these routine visits, the doctor noticed the early signs of incipient diabetes. Herm was alerted and modified his life accordingly. With the help of his doctor he has since learned to accept job reassignments that would otherwise have threatened to undermine Herm's value as an employee. He knows the limitations imposed by his age and condition and is gradually relinquishing his authority to a younger man who will be fully able to take over when Herm comes up for retirement. Herm's mental attitude toward retirement is good. He knows what he can and cannot do, and he knows what he wants out of life. He acquired this knowledge as a result of a constructive retirement program that was initiated before he began "aging in harness." His value to his boss and to the stockholders of his company has far exceeded the modest sums expended in keeping him in vertical health and productive. Not only has he been able to maintain high standards of job performance but he has been absent only four days out of eight years.

If Herm's employer had been content to handle Herm's potential health problem merely by setting up some sort of group medical costs indemnification plan, Herm would in all probability have acquired a full-blown case of depression. This would have come as a nasty surprise, perhaps with serious complications, and Herm would have found himself, despite his insurance coverage, deeply in debt to his physician and hospital. Moreover, he could have lost many days, maybe months, on the job, creating innumerable snarls in the shop schedule. Had he survived all this, it is difficult to estimate the magnitude of the problems that would inevitably have been triggered by the later emotional problem. Since it was in his nature to suppress such matters, the situation would not have come to light in the early stages. By degrees, Herm might have become an inefficient, senile, tendentious and thoroughly sick person. Just how much this would have meant in dollars and cents to his company cannot be determined with precision; but there is no doubt that Herm's rating as a liability would have exceeded his rating as an asset.

For the sake of the stockholders, for the sake of management, for the sake of the employed person himself, retirement programs should accent mantalent development and human maintenance. This philosophy needs special emphasis with regard to aging and retirement because it strikes at the heart of the growing social problem that is threatening to become the most perplexing one of modern times—that of the social waste of America's expanding population of senior citizens. This is a problem which will inevitably be placed on the shoulders of business, either as an organizational challenge or indirectly as a tax burden. Industry will gain by taking the initiative and choosing the former alternative.

The experience with Herman S. illustrates how a company's foresight in the anticipation and early recognition of problems can be beneficial to employer and employee alike. Since the nature and timing of the depredations of aging varies so greatly, planning and decisions must be individualized insofar as possible. The value to the company of some employees will last long beyond retirement age while that of others will decline well before an arbitrarily established age for retirement. If continued in their regular job, the latter may cause not only direct financial losses to a company due to illness as well as reduced productivity, but may trigger more extensive losses due to their adverse influence on fellow workers and on morale in general.

PREVENTIVE ADVICE FOR RETIREES

Whether overtaken by the handicaps of degenerative diseases prior to the conventional timing of retirement or anticipating their more or less inevitability in the future, the retiring employee may need clearly articulated health maintenance advice. Some companies already supply to their employees engagingly written illustrated booklets with helpful hints on weight and blood pressure control, advice on drinking, smoking, and exercise, as well as care of the eyes, ears, and teeth. These efforts could readily be extended to advice on coping with other potential limitations of aging such as arthritis, insomnia, etc (see Chapter 19).

INDIVIDUALIZING DECISIONS FOR RETIREMENT

While poorly timed retirement can be immensely costly to all concerned, forcing retirement prematurely at whatever age may deprive a company of highly developed expertise, experience, judgment, and loyalty. To bury such assets under a blanket retirement rule in the interest of avoiding favoritism and unjust discrimination is hardly in the interest of the employee, the company, or society at large. Individual judgments must be made because individuals differ so widely. It is time to develop standards for evaluating working ability based on physiologic, psychological, and sociologic criteria. Instead of retirement social and demographic data might be used to determine the most suitable occupations for older workers. The selection of early retirement for those for whom it is appropriate should then be based on a reliable understanding of the employee as a person.[253]

Equal opportunity and equality before the law do not translate into equal individual capability, equal motivation, or equal rate of slowing down with age. Companies need legal protection against challenges to enlightened personnel decisions just as employees need legal protection against unfair personnel practices. Discrimination, an expression of the high development of human mentality, need not therefore be scorned if fairly and conscientiously undertaken.

Experience with psychological and social influences on health and disease have provided ample evidence of the human and financial costs of indiscriminate application of rules and regulations. Retirement, therefore, in all of its aspects is big business, not to be administered by a prescribed booklet of personnel policies, but to be the subject of careful individualized thinking by the medical department and the top management.

Section IV: Responsibilities and Liabilities of Management

CHAPTER **12**

CORPORATE ROLE AND RESPONSIBILITIES

GUNNAR SEVELIUS

The right of citizens to life, liberty, and the pursuit of happiness does not necessarily imply a stress-free society but one in which there are choices and opportunities for individual initiative, one where stressful circumstances can provide a spur toward achievement and consequent personal satisfaction. As workers and citizens we must all respond to challenges. Some will be found fulfilling and others destructive. The circumstances in which corporate employees can pursue their goals are determined in part by the company and in part by the government. The purpose of this chapter is to outline the opportunities and responsibilities of corporations.

STRESS AT WORK

It has often been assumed that the workload itself is mainly responsible for stress-related diseases in industry. There is much evidence to the contrary, however. For example, in an investigation supported by the National Institute of Occupational Safety and Health (NIOSH), the work force at Lockheed Missiles and Space Co, Inc was tested for work-related stress by an independent scientific team from SRI, International. Two factors were tested: workload and work fit. Four hundred middle-management persons were randomly selected. Reports from their wives, coworkers, and themselves as well as numerous tests were collected and evaluated. The results revealed that neither particular occupation nor workload correlates with high blood pressure, nor with any other objective or subjective sign of a stress reaction. What mattered was how an employee's personality fitted into his particular work situation. Two personality extremes were recognized at either end of a spectrum. They corresponded closely to type A and type B behavioral patterns.[254]

The situations found to be stressful to each of these types of personalities are outlined in Table 12-1.[255] Since the sources of stress in the work environment for the two personality types were almost directly opposite from one another, it would be difficult to design a single work environment or organizational structure that would decrease stress in one group and not increase stress in the other. Fortunately no organization is characterized by a single work environment for everyone. Therefore, job assignments can reduce stress to a minimum by effecting a good fit between the worker and his/her environment and by educating (informing) the employee in what to expect in his job. An enlightened employer should, therefore, appreciate individual differences in employees and should support programs to assist the employees in finding a good fit within the organization and make them feel that it is safe and proper to seek such a fit. Thus it is in part the responsibility of the employee to recognize his personal needs and seek out employment which fits both his experience and his personality.

JOB FIT FOR THE HANDICAPPED

Specific medical problems may be faced in fitting handicapped people into suitable employment. The guiding rule is that the handicapped person should have an opportunity to fulfill his or her potential as an employee without jeopardizing the health of himself or his coworkers.[256]

Table 12-1
Stressful Situations in Type A and
Type B Personalities

Personality Traits	Source of Stress
Type A Autonomous, achievement oriented, aggressive, extroverted, confident, dominant, unconcerned about the physical features of the workplace; tend to suppress health concerns	Not enough personal involvement among workers; co-workers fail to take personal interest in one another
	Inadequate freedom to make decisions and to take initiative; excessive guidance and structure set forth by upper management
Type B Yielding in opinions, introverted, humble, expressing concern about health	Too much personal involvement among workers; co-workers take "excessive" personal interest in one another
	Inadequate guidance and structure provided by upper management; great deal of responsibility for decision-making.
	Crowded, too hot or too cold, poorly lit, outdated work environment

Each judgment must be made on an individual basis, since degree of disability varies so widely. Risk assessments should be based on the requirements of the job and the physical or mental limitations of the handicapped employee.

EMPLOYER ATTITUDES

No one will live all his adult life without a major crisis for himself or his family. When these situational life stresses come along it is important for immediate supervisors to communicate with their employees, to be supportive and understanding so that the stress may be minimized. Nothing will do more to hold a team together than a hand that reaches out in time of a personal crisis.

EMPLOYEE ATTITUDES

Low turnover of employees in a corporation means that most employees believe in the future of their employer. The employee feels that if he stays with the company he will be able to raise his family and perhaps someday retire with some financial security. Most workers do not ask for much more. This means that by far, most employees are on the side of the company in its effort to succeed—if for nothing else than for their own future financial security.

When this fundamental fact is realized, responsibility for both productivity and quality of work life, including work stress, can be spread throughout the work environment—to employees and management alike. Open discussions about how the quality of work life can be improved upon will relieve stress situations that could otherwise generate adversary relationships. Goals should be formulated with input from employees or their representatives so that everyone feels that his or her involvement is important.

A positive company spirit with all energy coordinated toward the same goal will not only make the organization more successful but, amazingly, less stressful.

SUMMARY

The question of responsibility for stress in the workplace is a complicated and emotional issue. As more facts become known it can be handled more rationally and with greater insight. The facts at present point to the conclusion that some responsibility rests with the worker, some with the corporation, and some with the government.

The corporation sets the stage on which all workers—labor as well as management—pursue happiness in their lives. To make this possible it is necessary for business enterprises—small and large—to recognize the differences in personality, age, sex, and attitudes, as well as limitations in physical and mental capacities. None is really handicapped but everyone is different. The uniqueness of each person allows for recognition of special assets; everyone should have the privilege of opportunity for and the recognition of his or her contributions.

CHAPTER **13**

INTERACTIONS AND SHARED RESPONSIBILITIES OF MANAGEMENT, MEDICAL DEPARTMENT, AND EMPLOYEES

BERTRAM D. DINMAN

The relationship of men and women in working groups inevitably contains the potential for discordance of individual goals and objectives especially when there are racial, ethnic, religious, or other social differences. Add to this the demands of the employer and there is a natural potential for stress generation. Management is most effective when corporate objectives are made clear, when job designs are coherent and logical, when relationships among coworkers and with supervisors are clearly delineated, and when limitations on freedom to act on individual initiative are explicit. On the other hand, when the job specification is vague, when there is ambiguity as to functional and administrative accountability, when productivity demands are unrealistic, or when responsibility is maximized in the face of little authority, stress responses among workers may ensue. Thus, failure to communicate can lead to avoidable impairments of performance and even of health of employees. Similarly, stress may appear when a worker's efforts or his capabilities are inadequately utilized, receive no recognition, or when there is no

136

constructive criticism for deficiencies, or no opportunity for a worker to express concerns or complaints. Finally, job insecurity associated with the threat of merger, concerns over the economic viability of older, high-cost operations, and anxiety stemming from low-cost foreign competition can contribute to the manifestation of stress responses. As pointed out in chapter 12, adequacy of the match between employee and job requirements is of great importance to job performance and health. Jobs which require coping with ambiguity are inappropriate for individuals who require structured, ordered settings. Conversely, the individual who tends to intellectualize or can cope with risk-taking is ill-suited to work at tasks of a routine nature. Again, collaboration with competent personnel managers can provide insights regarding job content and employee performance in the present job as well as in previous assignments. Changes in behavior and performance over time as variations occur in job assignment can afford clues regarding present employee complaints.

SIGNS AND SYMPTOMS OF STRESS IN THE WORK SETTING

Just as pathophysiologic aberrations produce signs and symptoms in the biological organism, similarly dysfunction of the individual components of the corporate body manifest certain organizational signs and symptoms. These include increased absenteeism, increased use of medical benefits, or alcohol abuse, deteriorating job performance, unnecessary risk-taking, and barely avoided injuries.

THE CORPORATE ROLE AND THAT OF THE MEDICAL OFFICER

Management has little right to intervene in the way an individual employee chooses to live or behave unless his behavior impairs job performance. Thus, even though an employee imbibes alcohol excessively while off the job, only when job performance is impaired may the employer intervene. It is, however, a management responsibility while acting in the company's best interests to deal expeditiously with sources of job-related stress and other adjustment problems of employees that may affect job performance and even health. In some instances, as when an employee comes to the medical department complaining of bodily symptoms, the medical officer may become involved directly in the stress problem. In other instances the physician may be consulted by a supervisor because he has become aware of the employee's symptoms or because he has noted frequent absences, tardiness, inadequate job performance, etc.

In case of direct contact with the employee, it is essential for the physician in industry to maintain full confidentiality as to the medical details. However, the physician should advise the employee that his supervisors must be made generally aware that an illness exists and that a recommendation for treatment has been made. It is then the responsibility of the employee to follow through with treatment. Permission is usually obtained from the employee to so inform the supervisor, especially if the patient is reassured that the *nature* of the treatment will *not* be communicated. In such instances the physician acts as a buffer for an employee with a health problem. The physician's further responsibility to management is to see that the patient complies with recommendations and to evaluate the efficacy of the therapy.

In those cases where the long-term prognosis is poor and job performance deteriorates, decisions as to disposition must be made. In such situations the employee's length of service, his value as a contributor, etc, must be taken into consideration. Where there has been faithful service or significant contributions, management and the physician will tend to exhaust the last resort before disability or retirement is recommended. The physician, who should be, and usually is involved in the decision-making process, must continue to protect the employee's confidentiality, while at the same time providing assessment of his ability and limitations in performance of his present assignment or another to which he might be adaptable.

CHAPTER 14

CORPORATE LIABILITY FOR OCCUPATIONAL MEDICINE PROGRAMS

STEPHEN R. PERMUT

During the twentieth century, due to statutory requirements,[257] labor negotiations, a corporate response to real and perceived judicial standards,[258] and in some cases corporate benevolence, many corporations of all sizes have instituted occupational (industrial) medicine programs. These programs are as variable in nature as are the reasons for their creation. However, in general, they represent the provision of health care to employees for the prevention or treatment of occupationally related disease (injury). The scope of the service provided may be limited to pre-employment physical examinations and a mechanism to transport employees to emergency facilities in case of injury, or they may extend to the provision of total health care for the employee and his family. Most occupational medicine programs, however, limit their care to only the employee and to diseases and injuries related to employment.

HISTORICAL PERSPECTIVE

Under common law there was no legal obligation by an employer to provide medical care for an employee who became injured or ill while at work. However, when it became obvious in the case of railroad workers that such a rule created an undue hardship, a number of courts modified the rule. They noted that railroad workers were often far from home and from their usual source of medical care and declared, therefore, that in the case of illness or injury at work the employer is obliged to provide either care or transport to an appropriate place for care. This rule became known as the emergency doctrine and subsequent judicial holdings in all but one jurisdiction (New York) have adopted this rule and have widened its scope to include all employers.[259]

Once this rule became well established a variety of types of health care provided by employers came into existence. Care provided in the setting of the workplace became known as occupational or industrial medicine. As different jurisdictions viewed the corporate liability for such programs differently, a complex body of law evolved concerning occupational medicine programs and related corporate liability.

Once there exists a duty to provide any level of care to employees the first sphere of corporate liability relates to the selection and/or retention of the responsible physician(s).

If an employer provides medical care without an established obligation to provide it, the employer need only exercise ordinary care in the selection and/or retention of his occupational physicians. If he does so he is not responsible for any malpractice of those physicians. Where there exists a statutory or judicial duty to provide occupational medical care, however, then, in general, there is a duty not only of reasonable care in the selection and retention of physicians but also under a theory of respondeat superior, a liability for the malpractice of such physicians. The rule is similar if the employer benefits directly from the delivery of such service to his employees. Such a benefit could even be the earning of a profit from a health fund derived from a deduction from the employees' wages.[260]

Except in the case of emergency, there is no requirement for the employer to care for nonoccupational illnesses. However, the definition of occupational diseases is expanding as more and more hazards are being recognized in the workplace. Not only is the era of "toxic torts" contributing to this expansion of liability, but many less obvious hazards are being suggested as being occupationally related and may result in additional corporate liability. For example, heart disease is generally held to be the result of the interplay of a number of hereditary, social (eg, smoking), and dietary factors. However, physical as well as emotional stress have also been shown to play a role. An employee under extreme physical or emotional stress on the job, who develops a heart attack, in a jurisdiction where an employer is under either a statutory or judicial duty to provide care for occupationally related illnesses, can reasonably expect to receive treatment provided by his employer. Thus, despite the fact that an employer is not obligated to provide care for nonoccupational illnesses, the distinction between occupational and nonoccupational illnesses is becoming less and less distinct, thereby expanding the scope of the duty of employers.[261]

In response to the expansion of workers' compensation statutes and other legislation, corporations have increasingly required physical examinations prior to employment. The pre-employment physical provides the first opportunity to evaluate the relationship between the corporate physician and the employee. It is clearly distinct from the usual doctor-patient relationship where the patient has selected the physician. In the case of a pre-employment physical examination when the corporation and not the patient (employee) has selected the physician, most courts have held that no doctor-patient relationship exists. Thus, the physician's only duty is to the corporation.[262] However, if the physician advises or treats the employee with reference to a condition discovered during such an examination, then a doctor-patient relationship has been established and the physician will be liable for providing an appropriate standard of care.[263] With regard to conditions discovered during a pre-employment physical examination the question arises as to the physician's duty to reveal such findings to the employee. Such a duty only exists if the physician discovers a condition of which he knows that the employee is unaware.[264] The same duty will exist to reveal findings made by occupational physicians of conditions discovered during preventive health care services provided by corporations, if they are unknown to the employee. In the case of preventive care provided to employees, it is clear that in some cases the information uncovered may be of a nature that creates liability to the corporation, as, for example, in the case of an employee acquiring a disease related to employment. Here it is the clear duty of occupational physicians to reveal to the employee an abnormal finding of which the employee is unaware.

Another situation in which corporations are increasingly finding themselves providing health care to employees is in the treatment of nonemergency job-related injuries. Since the vast majority of jurisdictions require the treatment of emergencies, many corporations have found it necessary to provide on-site medical services. Furthermore, since the distinction between a true emergency and nonemergency may not always be easily determined, either by physicians or the courts, many occupational medicine programs provide care for nonemergencies as well as emergencies. In addition, the workers' compensation statutes of several states require the provision of care for all job-related injuries.[265] The issue of corporate liability for the provision of such care is often difficult to determine in the light of differing workers' compensation statutes and the different corporate-physician relationships which exist.

In summary, it is clear that when a corporation endeavors to treat job-related injuries (or diseases) there is a duty beyond that of reasonable care in the selection and/or retention of the physicians, and there is a duty to provide a reasonable standard of care. This duty exists because once the occupational physician endeavors to treat the employee, a doctor-patient relationship is created and thus standard of care requirements will apply.[266] When a corporation further decides to provide care for non-emergent, non-occupational illnesses a similar theory of the establishment of both a doctor-patient relationship and liability will exist.

THE LIABILITY OF THE CORPORATION
VERSUS THAT OF THE PHYSICIAN

Separating corporate from physician liability in the occupational medicine setting is often difficult. If liability rests with the corporation due to alleged malpractice by an occupational medicine physician, then, by virtue of statutory provision, only the proof of injury will be necessary under workers' compensation statutes and not proof of fault. If, on the other hand, the liability rests with the physician, and the physician is not deemed to be a coemployee under the workers' compensation statute of the jurisdiction involved, then the physician's liability will depend not only upon the proof of injury but also upon all the elements which will be necessary to prove that the injury resulted from the physician's negligence.[267] Similarly, the level of recovery for the employee for the injury will be limited to statutory recovery under the workers' compensation statute, whereas if the recovery is a common law recovery against the physician, a full recovery based upon proof of damages may be obtained.[267]

The determination of corporate v physician liability will depend upon many factors. Among them will be whether or not the workers' compensation statute for the jurisdiction involved contains a provision for immunity of coemployees against third party suits. Even if there is such a provision, often the judicial interpretation of that provision or the court's interpretation of the legislative intent of the entire statute may be such as to exclude physicians. The reasons given are several. Among them are that the writers of workers' compensation statutes, when providing immunity from third party suits to coemployees, were not contemplating the extension to employees whose professional responsibilities are far removed from the usual tasks of coemployees in the industrial setting.[268] A second reason given is that the coemployees given workers' compensation immunity are under the direct control of the corporation (the common law control test used for determination of respondeat superior) but that physicians employed by corporations are not. This distinction becomes less clear in the case of larger occupational medicine programs where there is a medical director who sets corporate policy for the conduct of the physician's activity, thereby establishing a level of corporate control. In such situations some courts have found there to be sufficient corporate control for the coemployee exemption of the workers' compensation statute to apply to physicians as well.[269]

Another set of factors which has influenced the corporate v the third party liability of occupational physicians depends upon the specific circumstances of his employment. He may be full-time, salaried, with no other outside professional activities; full-time, salaried, with other outside professional activities; full-time, fee-for-service, with or without other outside professional activities; part-time, salaried; part-time, fee-for-service; independent contractor, or a private practitioner recommended by the corporation. Each of these situations has been met with findings of either corporate or physician liability depending upon the jurisdiction. However, the greater the appearance of the physician as a corporate employee, who is functioning within the scope of his employment by the corporation and for the benefit of the corporation, the greater the chance that the court will determine the presence of coemployee status for the physician.

An additional rationale under which third party liability of an occupational physician has been found is the court's interpretation that the provision of third party immunity under workers' compensation statutes was intended to protect low-paid coemployees and not high-paid corporate physicians. This argument does not take into account the third party immunity available to other high-paid corporate executives under workers' compensation statutes.[270]

Another judicial rationale which has been used in some jurisdictions to deny coemployee immunity to occupational medicine physicians is that to do so would encourage negligent care by corporate physicians.[271] However, this argument does not consider the fact that such negligent care would still be compensated under the corporation's workers' compensation insurance coverage. A corporation whose physicians practiced negligently would establish for itself a higher experience rate for such insurance coverage and its rates for that coverage would rise. Thus, as with any on-the-job injury, corporations are encouraged to reduce negligent performance in all spheres so that their insurance costs are as low as possible.

A final criterion which has been used to determine the liability of the corporation rather than the physician for occupational medicine services depends upon the site where the services are rendered. Thus, if the occupational health services are provided in a clinic or hospital that is open to the public as well as to corporate employees, then the services are viewed by the courts of some jurisdictions as health care services provided in a traditional setting with traditional doctor-patient relationships and, thus, common law physician liability applies to any medical malpractice. On the other hand, if the occupational medicine service is delivered in a setting in which only occupational medicine services to corporate employees are provided, then corporate liability under workers' compensation statutes is deemed to exist for any additional injury resulting from the treatment itself.[272]

There have developed two opposing judicial standards with regard to the concept of coemployee status of occupational medicine physicians. In many jurisdictions the courts interpret the legislative intent of their respective workers' compensation statutes literally. If at the time of the alleged malpractice the physician was performing in the status of a corporate employee, the court will view him as such and grant him the coemployee immunity granted by many workers' compensation statutes. In such situations the injured employee's exclusive remedy will be limited to the statutory recovery designated by the workers' compensation statute of that jurisdiction. On the other hand, the court might be one of those following the so-called dual capacity doctrine as described in *Duprey v Shane.*[273] The dual capacity doctrine views a corporate physician as serving in two distinct capacities: one as an employee of the corporation, and another as a physician whose primary responsibility is to his patients, the corporation's employees. The jurisdictions following the dual capacity doctrine hold that the occupational medicine physician's role as a coemployee is clearly subordinate to his role as an independent professional. Thus, the dual capacity doctrine denies these physicians the protection of the statutory remedies provided under workers' compensation statutes.

There are multiple arguments favoring either doctrine. Those finding the physicians qualifying as coemployees rely primarily upon the legislative intent of the workers' compensation statute of their jurisdiction. Those courts, referring to the fact that in many states coemployee immunity provisions have been added by amendment, hold that if the legislatures had desired that only certain employees be so protected, they would have specified which employees should possess such immunity. Further, they hold that if physicians are not intended to have such immunity, that the legislature should so amend their statutes.

The courts upholding the dual capacity doctrine contend that the physicians' responsibilities to their patients (the corporate employees) transcend their responsibilities to the corporation. Next they find that corporate physicians do not participate in the employer-employee quid pro quo of workers' compensation statutes in that the physicians have little chance of being injured by a fellow employee and, thus, do not relinquish any rights through the coemployee provision.

In addition, they feel that to provide coemployee protection to occupational medicine physicians would encourage physician malpractice, since the physicians would have no personal liability. Those favoring coemployee status point out that corporations go to great lengths to promote job safety in order to maintain low claims records for their workers' compensation insurance policies. It would follow that corporations would similarly encourage competent delivery of occupational health care services to similarly limit claims. A final argument used in support of the dual capacity doctrine is that preventing third party recovery from malpracticing occupational medicine physicians prevents full recovery for the employee's injury, since workers' compensation recoveries are statutory, do not cover pain and suffering, and are generally limited to some proportion of the employee's lost wages plus medical expenses.[274,275] However, it does not appear that extension of liability to some portion of the corporation's higher paid employees, ie, physicians, is the appropriate approach to the limitation of workers' compensation statutes. It would seem more appropriate for the statutory recoveries to be made more realistic or for physicians to be excluded as coemployees depending on the preference of the respective legislatures.

PROXIMATE CAUSE OF INJURY BY OCCUPATIONAL MEDICINE PROGRAMS

When the medical care rendered results in aggravation of a job-related illness or injury there is corporate liability whether or not malpractice by an occupational medicine physician is involved and whether or not the corporation was negligent in the selection of the physician,[276] and even if the treatment was rendered by a noncorporate physician of the employee's choice. Such liability will be compensated under the workers' compensation statute of the appropriate jurisdiction.

In the case of nonoccupational illness or injury, however, damages even for malpractice will not be covered under the appropriate workers' compensation statute but a common law action can be pursued against the employer and/or the physician. The determination in such cases as to whether it is the corporation or the physician who is to be held liable is based first upon the determination of whether or not the corporation was negligent in the selection of the physician. If the corporation was negligent in the selection of the physician, then the holdings have been against the corporation. Such was the case in *Smith v Mallinckrodt,*[277] where a corporation allowed a retired physician who was working for them as a clerk to treat employees for nonoccupationally related illnesses. When there is no negligence in selecting the physician, the corporation may still be held liable if the court construes that the corporation has profited or in some other way benefited from the provision of health care services to its employees and/or their families. This was the case in *Owens v Atlantic Coast Lumber Corp,*[278] where the corporation deducted monthly sums from the employees for the provision of such services and derived profit from such deductions. If, on the other hand, there has been no negligence in the selection of the physician and no profit realized by the corporation, it will be the physician against whom a common law recovery will be permitted.[279]

RESPONSIBILITY FOR DAMAGES

Whether or not an employer will be required to compensate an employee for damages incurred in connection with the treatment of an injury may depend greatly on the statutory provisions of the appropriate jurisdiction's workers' compensation statute and the judicial decisions interpreting those statutes.

In many jurisdictions if an employee has elected to receive workers' compensation for an injury sustained, and later discovers that he was a victim of malpractice, he will be barred from recovering from the physician who treated him for the injury. This can present a dilemma since in most cases the statute of limitations for filing a workers' compensation claim is considerably shorter than that allowed for a medical malpractice action.[279] Other jurisdictions only bar such third party actions if the claim made under workers' compensation included the damages for medical malpractice.

In some jurisdictions where third party suits are allowed, the employee must release the corporation from all workers' compensation claims before a third party suit can be entered against the negligent physician. In still other jurisdictions what amounts to a double recovery is allowed. That is, the employee may proceed with the workers' compensation claim against the corporation for both the lost wages and medical expenses for the original injury and any aggravation for medical malpractice as well as against the physician in a common law tort action for any damages sustained as a result of the malpractice. Some of the jurisdictions allowing employees both avenues of recovery also allow subrogation by the corporation from the employee for damages which the corporation paid the employee for injuries sustained as a result of the malpractice which the employee recovers from the physician in a third party suit.[279] In still other jurisdictions the corporation is allowed to sue the physician to recover the portion of the damages it paid for medical malpractice once the employee elects his exclusive remedy under workers' compensation.[279]

DEFENSES

Except where the employee's injury occurs as the result of the intentional conduct of the employer's activities, defenses are of little concern since most corporate liability in such cases is covered under no-fault workers' compensation statutes. Since only proof of injury is required for recovery and not fault, the use of legal defenses to liability is unnecessary. However, where common law rather than statutory recovery applies, as in the case of intentional conduct on the part of the employer or where a third party suit for medical malpractice is allowed against an occupational medicine physician, then the usual defenses such as assumption of risk and contributory or comparative negligence may apply.

INTENTIONAL INJURIES BY OCCUPATIONAL PHYSICIANS WITHIN THE "SCOPE" OF THEIR EMPLOYMENT

Intentional injuries (torts) in an occupational setting may consist of actions on the part of a physician where the proper care of the patient is compromised by an effort to protect the company. Some workers' compensation statutes include intentional torts within the scope of employment but most do not.[280] Where such torts were not contemplated by the workers' compensation statute, common law recovery has been permitted. In one such case, the physician involved was held culpable of malicious malpractice because he attempted to protect the corporation from having to pay the statutory recovery to which the employee was entitled.[281] In other cases, deceit by the corporation or the occupational medicine physician was the basis for the intentional nature of the injury. In one case the corporation withheld information regarding the hazards of its product from their occupational medicine physicians, resulting in the continued exposure and injury to the employee.[282] In another case, where both a corporate physician and a social worker misrepresented to a worker his ability to return to work with resulting injury to the employee and his family, the court found that such activity was not protected by the workers' compensation statute of the jurisdiction and that there was both corporate and third party common law liability.[283]

Thus, when a corporation, attempting to control the professional activities of its physicians, becomes responsible for inappropriate care to its employees, it may well be found to have inflicted intentional injury upon them. On the other hand, when physicians care for corporate employees in such a manner as to place the interest of the corporation above that of their employee patients, even though they may have been accorded statutory protection under the jurisdiction's workers' compensation statute, they too may be found liable for intentional injury under a common law recovery.

CONCLUSIONS

The great variety of occupational medicine programs that exist today are matched by the variability of the workers' compensation statutes in different jurisdictions across the country. This has led to a complex body of law concerning corporate liability and the liability of their occupational medicine physicians. Thus, it is difficult for anyone involved to predict with certainty whether liability will be found purely under the statutory provisions of the workers' compensation laws of the jurisdiction or through a common law suit for negligence or some combination of the two. Corporations and/or occupational physicians are best advised to have liability insurance coverage beyond that which is provided by the corporation's workers' compensation policy. Employees who have sustained injury due to negligent health care received from an occupational medicine program should review the judicial holdings in their jurisdiction to know whether their right of recovery will be limited by the workers' compensation statute or whether they can instead or in addition seek a common law recovery by bringing suit against the corporation and/or the occupational physician.

CHAPTER **15**

THE CONCEPT AND PRACTICE OF STRESS MANAGEMENT

BONNIE C. SEAMONDS

Many, if not most business organizations have productivity and health problems related to occupational stress. When there is a significant degree of impairment of individual and corporate productivity, special efforts to mitigate stress and its negative effects may be warranted. Beyond that, a prime objective of stress management programs is to counteract the effects of inevitable stresses by an effort to enhance individual and group morale and thus to strengthen the individual's ability to cope. The morale of a group of workers often determines whether pressures to produce become an agreeable challenge or a disabling handicap. Factors that adversely affect morale include work overload, poor job fit, role conflict, and role ambiguity. An especially prominent factor is failure of recognition by supervisors of the workers' efforts.[284]

Segments of the work population should be sampled to get first-hand information about work stress. Supervisors on the shop floor or first-line managers are often the best people to sample as they experience stress from the nature of the job, the mandates of senior management, and from subordinates who present their own unique problems. We know that one of the most stressful jobs is in the management of people rather than managing assets. It is the first-line manager's job to forge a work team from a group of individuals who have their own experiences, personalities, and personal goals. The manager must help these employees define the work task, set mutual goals, and work in a systematic way to accomplish these goals. No mean feat!

There are many kinds of measurements for occupational stressors. Kahn et al[285] have developed a 15-question scale for measuring work stress. This scale can be administered to any level of work group. Their questionnaire looks at role conflict, role ambiguity, work overload, recognition received, advancement issues, and work/family balance. The social readjustment rating scale of Holmes and Rahe[286] is another measure for change both at work and at home for 12-month periods. The number of changes occurring in an individual's life has been found to correlate positively with the incidence of stress-related illnesses.

Simple measures directed at educating the managers and increasing their awareness of signs of stress among employees may be all that some companies require to head off unproductive morale problems. Establishment of hygienic programs of exercise, relaxation, and diet as well as counseling about smoking, alcohol, and drug abuse have also been found profitable in some companies. Others, after careful introspection, may elect to institute a more formal stress management plan. They may rely on their medical department to initiate such a process.

The first step in program development aimed to assess and manage stress-related problems is to acquire or design educational materials to increase the general understanding of stress—what it is, and how it can affect health and job performance. This information is crucial for corporate decision-makers as they will decide to give or not to give their support to the education of employees in stress management.

The next step is to evaluate the needs of the corporation and the needs of the individual workers.

Stresses may arise from (1) the kind of work being done, eg, very aggressive marketing and selling as in a high-tech company; (2) the norms of the organization—where a chief executive officer (CEO) may value a high-pressure and rapidly changing environment; (3) management styles where a highly competitive environment may create intense pressure. All three factors can be operating at the same time. In one large oil company, for example, prospective employees are expected to respond in the affirmative to the statement, "I work well under pressure."

Where pressure is valued as a motivator it may be difficult to obtain executive commitment to stress management programs.

Success in the development and ultimate utilization of stress management programs depends on the following:

1. Educational materials to increase awareness and understanding of occupational stress throughout the organization. These may include films and other prepackaged health promotion materials, and articles in newsletters and bulletins.
2. Identification of needs.
3. Executive commitment to support the programs.
4. A cost-effective in-service training program.
5. Available resources for referral when needed.
6. A follow-up program for evaluation and to monitor change.

Executive commitment to stress management is indispensable; without it programs fail. Individual employees who go through a stress management program may benefit, but the organization will not appreciably change.

A corporate inventory of the following health benefits can be useful in assessing needs:

1. Mental health insurance coverage
2. Regular health examinations
3. In-house medical services
4. Risk reduction and prevention (programs for hypertension, weight control, relaxation training, physical fitness)

5. Health promotion efforts

6. Counseling services

It may be advisable in certain organizations not to label stress management programs as such. While medical personnel may be sympathetic to stress-related symptoms and illnesses of employees, line executives may not be as they adhere to the myth that "admitting to experiencing stress implies that one cannot handle his job." Getting help to affected employees in this kind of setting may necessitate finding euphemisms for the programs such as "managing change" or "human resource maintenance" that do not directly challenge this myth.

Services that may already be in place in some corporations can contribute to the alleviation of stress. For example, many compaies have job performance and appraisal systems which are used to decide on merit increases in pay. Such appraisals also can be used as a coaching tool for the manager to help employees learn to solve their own problems. The yearly appraisal should not, however, be a substitute for more or less continuous or frequent monitoring of an employee's motivation, job performance, attitude, and task completion.

Once the desirability of instituting a stress management program has been accepted by the company and the needs peculiar to that organization have been identified, it may be appropriate to screen the employees for more specific information on which to design the program itself.

SCREENING

Screening procedures are many and varied. In one corporation, for example, an occupational questionnaire is administered and scored for every employee who participates in a periodic health examination program in the corporate medical department.[287] Other corporations use a paper and pencil test to measure job stress. It can be administered to all employees who utilize the employee assistance program.

Both low and high scores should be identified because those exposed to high on-job stress due to work overload, lack of recognition, etc, have been shown to develop similar symptoms to those who score on the low end which may indicate poor job fit, boredom, and underutilization.[288]

Having done the screening, the next step is an individual interview to pinpoint more precisely levels of stress, kinds of stressors, adaptive and maladaptive coping skills, and physical and psychological symptoms. During the interview an individual stress management plan can be fashioned to reduce the effects of stress and to promote optimal health practices such as regular exercise, relaxation breaks, and proper nutrition. Referrals to available resources, especially to a seminar in stress management, may be especially useful. Because some of the information obtained is personal, maintaining strict confidentiality is important. For this reason, it is appropriate to have an outside consultant conduct the interviews. An interview format requiring only 20 minutes, which has been used very successfully in a large financial institution with both domestic and international locations, is outlined below:

Interview Outline:
1. Presenting problem
2. Relevant history
3. Health status (including habits)
4. Stress symptoms
5. Life balance
   a. Nutritional status
   b. Exercise program
   c. Sleep pattern
   d. Recognition
   e. Environment
   f. Support systems (family, work)
   g. Leisure time
6. Major life changes—number and kind
   a. Death (spouse, family, friend)

   b. Marriage, separation, divorce
   c. Community problems (work, spouse, family)
   d. Change in health (family, self)
   e. Change in financial status (up, down)
   f. Sexual difficulties
   g. Birth of a child
   h. Problems with children
   i. Relocation
  7. Time management
  8. Referral
  9. Stress score

Presenting Problem

What is going on in the employee's life and in the corporation? What is the source of the stress that he/she is currently experiencing? Are these stressors due to a faulty management style, attitude problems, or are they intrinsic to the job itself?

Here the interviewer is looking for the employee's awareness and understanding of work stressors and their effects. It is important to uncover "macho" attitudes and beliefs about work stress: "I can handle anything," "Nothing bothers me," "It is not okay to admit to having stress problems in this organization." The interviewer should recognize that it may not be politically wise in certain organizations to admit to work stress problems. He should therefore assure the employee that the content of the interview will be kept strictly confidential.

Relevant History

Of special concern are personal status loss from a demotion, a lateral move, or a decrease in responsibility. Other concerns may result from ambiguous assignments or overfrequent changes such as reassignments and new bosses. Is the employee succeeding in meeting his own goals? How does his perception of the work compare to what his supervisors tell him?

Health Status

How healthy has the employee been in the past year? Does he/she have frequent colds and the flu? Are there recent behavior changes such as increases in smoking, overeating, alcohol intake, or changes in sleep patterns? Maintaining good health and good health habits affords protection against the strains and pressures of work. Indeed, "rejoicing as a strong man to run a race," the healthy, optimistic employee may thrive on the stresses of work.

Stress symptoms Often employees do not relate their symptoms to the kind of stress they are experiencing. There should be careful inquiry as to headaches, gastric problems, high blood pressure, and sleep disturbances as well as psychological symptoms such as irritability, withdrawal, and loss of sense of humor.

Life Balance

How is the employee managing his life with regard to apportioning time and energy to work, family, and self? Does he examine and assess his priorities periodically? What motivates him to maintain a high level of output in his work as well as to manage people effectively? Does the work environment offer opportunities to further his skills and ambitions? Does the physical environment have adequate lighting, heating, air circulation, privacy needs, etc? Does the employee have friends, family, or bosses to whom he/she can turn for emotional support, confirmation of self-esteem, the discussion of problems, and receiving feedback? Is he maintaining interests outside of work (community affairs, hobbies, sports, etc)? Often when interviewing in this area, serious gaps can be discovered, and a plan developed to round out these areas.

For example, a 58-year-old executive who suffered personal status loss by being shifted laterally by a new young boss had become increasingly bitter, especially knowing he had to "stick it out" for 2 more years until retirement. The interview revealed that he had not made any plans for retirement and had few outside interests. His distress was considerably ameliorated when he agreed to get involved in preretirement planning and to pursue some specific outside interests.

Major Life Event

Holmes and Rahe[286] devised a questionnaire to assess amounts of stress in various aspects of a person's life such as family problems, health, financial problems, and other adjustment problems. Some of the interview questions are derived from their work. The benefits of the interview when focused on these matters depend heavily on the skills of the interviewer and his/her ability to put the employee at ease and encourage his need to share his concerns.

Time Management

How well is the employee managing time? Does he/she need training in delegating, coaching, confronting, negotiating, or goal setting? "I don't have time to (exercise, eat properly, etc)." These comments are more often than not a result of lack of skill in organization rather than lack of available time. In this part of the interview some assessment is made of the kinds of unproductive stress generated by inadequate skills, and how this lack of skills can create stress for the employee, the boss, and their subordinates. For example, a 46-year-old executive who was working 14-hour days was frustrated with his job and finding much of it monotonous. It was learned during the interview that he was not delegating even routine tasks. He believed that he could best do the job himself and was unwilling to compromise by sharing his workload. Additional training in delegating and time management was offered and accepted with gratifying results.

Summary

During the course of the interview described, a plan can be developed with an employee to recognize what his/her needs are and how he/she can best meet those needs in order to reduce the impact of identified stressors. It is clear that employees can manage much of their own health care by utilizing available resources.

Follow-up

A follow-up is indicated to assess the benefits of the interview, the success of the employee's efforts to manage his own stress, and the appropriateness of any referrals made. The information can be obtained through questionnaires or telephone calls some time after the interview.

OTHER OPTIONS

Stress management programs can be conducted with small groups of executives[289] where self-assessment and small group/work can enhance learning and retention. General and specific aspects of stress management can be discussed and experienced in a group setting. It is crucial, however, to build into the structure time for each participant to meet with the trainer on a one-to-one basis. It is essential that the employee feel free to express himself without fear or loss of image. It is evident that a trainer should have diverse and comprehensive skills in consulting, psychology, and interviewing with certainly some medical background.

Program design should be based on the needs of particular participants. That is why "canned" programs in stress management are not recommended. One relaxation method may not be applicable to a whole group of employees. There are, however, commonalities in the area of stress management training that can be taught to most participants. Some general concepts include:

1. Helping the employee to understand himself by learning to assess strengths and weaknesses with regard to coping skills
2. Identification of work and personal stressors
3. Identification of impact of stressors
4. Clarification of personal and professional goals
5. Recognition of symptoms of stress reactions
6. Understanding coping skills—both adaptive and maladaptive
7. Learning to exert control over changes by pacing himself
8. Establishing priorities
9. Setting realistic goals
10. Managing time effectively
11. Getting the skills training needed—both professional and personal
12. Developing a flexible style
13. Evaluating and setting priorities periodically
14. Learning to play, to relax, and to put things in proper perspective
15. Developing personal coping skills such as exercise programs, relaxation methods, exercise, proper diet, and social networks

The objectives of a stress management program from an occupational point of view are:

1. Helping the executive maximize productivity from others, both peers and subordinates, by understanding what stress is and how it can affect productivity.
2. Assisting employees in coping more effectively with work and personal stressors by developing the ap-

propriate coaching skills and by making appropriate referrals to available resources.

3. Incorporating behaviors and attitudes designed to minimize unproductive stress into one's management style through skills training efforts.

Working with small groups of employees is more cost-effective than one-on-one experiences. With the appropriate precautions stated previously, a combination of both individual interviewing and group experience is most effective. The most efficient use of time for stress management training is the modular approach where groups of employees meet for several hours over a 2-week period culminating in individual interviews. Participants complete homework in the form of self-assessment exercises, try out new behaviors at the work site, and report back at each group stress management session. Off-site meetings are generally favored by participants to minimize interruptions. Adherence to the criteria mentioned in this chapter, with particular emphasis on comprehensive needs analysis at the outset to determine the real need for such a program, should result in a responsible and relevant learning experience.

4. Proliferation of the message and the benefits through layers of executives, supervisors, and workers.

A benefit can be multiplied through the behavior of the boss to his subordinates at every level of the organization. His education in stress management should include his communication with his subordinates, his ability to detect and deal with problems, and his understanding of the needs, aspirations, and capabilities of others so that his assignment of tasks and his expectations can be wise and realistic.

Meeting these objectives will require the full backing of the corporate decision-makers and their commitment to a company-wide emphasis on education in the detection and effective management of stress among all levels of employees.

CHAPTER 16

COMMUNICATING WITH
THE EMPLOYEE AS
A PATIENT

STEWART WOLF

To achieve effective communication with employees a company's medical department must overcome the handicap of its identification with management. The most obvious problem to avoid is confusing overlap between the domain of the personnel officer and that of the medical director. While pre-employment screening by the personnel department properly includes questions about work record, emotional stability, family solidarity, habits, aptitudes, and intelligence, and while these data may properly be made available to the medical department, the medical records must remain privileged and confidential. The employee must be protected in a convincing way against real or imagined hazards of censure or betrayal. No device to assure the confidentiality of a company's records is as effective and convincing as is personal trust merited by, and accorded to the medical staff. Beyond this the major determinant of effective evaluation of symptoms is the skill of the interviewer in encouraging his patient to talk freely and in interpreting what is said.

Donald Ross in his book, *Practical Psychiatry for Industrial Physicians*,[290] provides useful guidance to the industrial physician for this important phase of his examination and cites the work of Elton Mayo and others who have written about the principles and techniques of interviewing and counseling in the industrial setting. The proper approach differs little from that appropriate to medical practice in general. For a fairly detailed treatment of the subject, the reader is referred to chapter 4, "Talking with the patient" in Wolf and Goodell's *Behavioral Science in Clinical Medicine.*[291] A few quotations from that work may serve to outline the major technical features.

THE SETTING AND CIRCUMSTANCES OF COMMUNICATION

To talk effectively with a patient, the setting and circumstances must be appropriate and conducive to good communication. Just as one cannot listen adequately to a heart beat if the patient is wearing a coat and shirt, or if there is noise from passing traffic, so one needs a suitable situation for an adequate interview. Privacy and comfort are fundamental to the setting. The room should be quiet, the chairs comfortable, and the session free of interruption.

The precise manner in which the physician greets his patient is a matter of personal preference. However, many physicians in their desire not to be austere or forbidding, may assume a casual or jaunty air with cigarette in hand and feet on the desk. Such exaggerated and unbecoming informality is usually ineffective, if indeed not actually disconcerting to a patient who hopes his problems will be taken seriously. The goal of an interview is to understand your patient as a person. Thus, the crux of good communication is to find out what makes this person in front of you what he is.

The Approach

It is the first rule of good communication that the physician and associated health professionals appear unhurried. Success or failure in communication often depends heavily upon the patient's initial impression of the physician. Repeatedly, one hears patients say of a physician, "He's such a busy man. I didn't want to burden him with my troubles," or "He didn't have time to talk to me, he was only interested in my cough." The physician who, even unintentionally, has given his patient such an impression has placed himself at a disadvantage and has perhaps denied himself important diagnostic data.

Other statements frequently made by patients who have left a physician are, "I was a little afraid of him," or, "He didn't seem interested," or "He seemed to have troubles of his own." Such remarks imply, of course, a defect in the attitude of the physician who failed to put the patient at ease and inspire his confidence. Good communication is no mere technical matter. The physician's personal qualities determine his ability to gain his patient's confidence and win his cooperation.

The History

A careful history with special attention to the sequence of events is probably the most powerful diagnostic tool. Its use requires highly developed skill in interviewing. Unfortunately it is currently popular for physicians to place little emphasis on history-taking and rely instead on questionnaires and structured interviews often administered by the nurse, secretary, or assistant. Such standardized lists of questions or topics to be covered do, however, have the advantage of protecting against incompleteness in data-gathering and of providing for greater precision in the description of symptoms, their setting, and antecedent events. Moreover, relative uniformity of data-gathering in this fashion makes possible analysis by computer and meaningful comparisons among patients. Computer programs that correlate pertinent symptoms and signs and indicate therefrom probable categories of disease or the existence of emotional conflicts and depression are helpful if they are used to suggest further probing inquiry by the skillful physician. When, however, reliance on data from prescribed questions supersedes, instead of supplements, the penetrating interview, the advantages fade, crucial leads are never pursued, and potential understanding is replaced by confusion. A device that may be of help to the physician in organizing data and correlating symptoms with events and emotional reactions is Adolf Meyer's life chart (see Figure 16-1).

It is usually easier to gather data regarding the social history, the personal lives of patients, if questions are asked as they seem pertinent in the context of "present illness," "past history," or "occupation, education, and family history" rather than in the separate category, "personal history." The objective is to find out about the patient as a person in his own particular environment. Specifically, one tries to learn how he looks at life, how he sees himself in relation to other people, what his aspirations and goals were and are, and what his values and standards, his vulnerabilities and sensitivities are. These constitute a revealing profile of a person.

A life story means little as a recital of events unless one understands the peculiar significance of the events to the particular patient concerned. Much of this information cannot be gathered from answers to direct questions. Instead it must often be inferred from the patient's account of his life story, the organization of his life style, and the kind of decisions he has made. The details of the events themselves are important only insofar as they indicate something about the person by the way they were handled. You could not tell much about a piece of music if you were simply told what notes were used in it. It is the arrangement of notes, the timing, the modulations, and the emphasis, among others, that make up the character of the composition. Similarly, it is the way in which a person leads his life, not so much a description of events, that tells you the information you will need in a social history. An account of specific conflicts and overt emotional experiences is useful but not sufficient. There is a relatively limited number of emotional conflicts, and they plague nearly

CASE V

NAME: The Girl Who Panted   HOSPITAL # 352919
HEREDITY: Alcoholic Father, Feeble Minded Mother
SIBLINGS: Third of Six   DATE: 1938

YEAR	MEDICAL DATA	ILLNESS	SOCIAL DATA	AGE
1915			Born in Maine	0
1916	Convulsions Pneumonia		Fell in cesspool	1
1917	Mumps		Brother born	2
1918				3
1919	Chickenpox			4
1920				5
1921	Measles			6
1922	Otitis Nail biting		Began school	7
1923				8
1924	Fractured arm, Sleep walking and talking.		Brother born	9
1925				10
1926	Menarche Strangling feelings			11
1927	Minor injury to knee Crutches for 3 months		Story of rape incident	12
1928	Menstrual cramps		Seventh grade	13
1929	Knee and crutches again			14
1930	Tonsillectomy Arm bandaged		Falling off at school	15
1931	Fainting spell		Scared by drunken father	16
1932	Vomiting "Nervous breakdown"		Father died Stopped school. Earns $4 a week	17
1933	"Kicked by a child" and on crutches		Another rape story. Earns $5 a week	18
1934	Fainting, blindness, paralysis		Caring for sick grandmother	19
1935	Headaches Choreic movements		Brother married Divine healing	20
1936	"Tetany" "Chorea"		Caring for asthmatic patient M.G.H.	21
1937	Improved		Discharged, back at work	22
1938	Hospital for tetany		Working again	23

Figure 16-1 Cobb's modification of Adolf Meyer's life chart, citing, under social data, "fell in cesspool." (Reproduced with permission from White BV: *Stanley Cobb.* Charlottesville, Va, University of Virginia Press, 1984.)

everyone more or less. Likewise, there are relatively few emotions or feeling states, and these are also experienced by nearly everyone from time to time. The significant item to be sought is the patient's attitude or *Weltanschauung,* the way the world looks to him and the way he sees himself in relation to it and its inhabitants. To achieve this kind of information, questioning must be skillful and answering made easy for the patient. Here, the physician adapts himself and his line of inquiry to what he knows of the patient's intellectual level and sociocultural background. It is impressive to note how much a perceptive history-taker can learn about a person in half an hour. This presupposes, of course, that the doctor himself does very little of the talking. Questions should be of a prompting nature, sympathetic, with a tone of interest but no excitement, no overt curiosity, and above all no attitude of surprise or disapproval.

Effective treatment in the form of talking with the patient does not require adherence to any specific doctrine or theory. Nor does it necessarily require couches, certificates, or other professional office trappings. It does, however, require experience and a commitment on the part of the physician to understand his patient as a person together with careful training in, and a full appreciation of, the diagnostic and therapeutic use of the interview.

The foregoing chapters have emphasized the cost effectiveness of good morale and the importance of considering employees as individuals as a major element in morale building. They have also called attention to the importance of tapping the full capacity of the patients with social and emotional problems since, as Page[3] and others had recognized, such individuals when properly assigned may be among the most outstanding performers. The present chapter has emphasized the skill and sophistication needed to achieve effective communication with individuals, and to make the necessary judgments of the patient as a person.

CHAPTER 17

THE CONTROL OF
ABSENTEEISM

BONNIE C. SEAMONDS

Occupational medicine has a growing responsibility to help employees stay well. There is an increasing need in the workplace for procedures to assess, educate and assist employees in an effort to promote optimal health. Gherman[292] discussed the corporate sector's unique capacity to promote awareness of illness prevention and to take an active role in providing guidelines for employees to better manage much of their own health care.

A recent study released by the Bureau of National Affairs[293] showed that approximately 50% of worker absences can be avoided by corporations attending to employee needs—both physical and emotional. The study also showed that there is a positive correlation between absences and the attitudes of employees to their superiors. The results, based on responses from 137 personnel executives throughout the country, point to a need for illness prevention efforts in industry. Only one fourth of the firms responding had developed new programs such as job enrichment, worker participation programs, and occupational health programs (which may or may not include stress management).

The research described here was undertaken to determine if the illness absentee rate of corporate employees could be effectively decreased by intervention through a health evaluation interview—a new prevention program. One objective was to promote concepts of optimal health in the workplace among individuals who were not aware of these concepts or who were evidencing maladaption to work stressors. An initial study of 500 employees was replicated with nearly identical results.[287]

The original study and the replication covered 1000 employees in a large financial institution, ranging from senior and middle management personnel to support personnel. The interview was done in conjunction with periodic medical examinations in the medical department, where 4000 medical examinations are done yearly.

Embedded in the medical history were 15 questions related to job stress, particularly questions concerning role ambiguity, role overload, recognition factors, and job suitability.

Job Stress Questions*

1. How often do you feel that you have too little authority to carry out your responsibilities?
2. How often do you feel unclear just what the scope and responsibilities of your job are?
3. How often do you not know what opportunities for advancement or promotion exist for you?
4. How often do you feel that you have too heavy a work load, one that you could not possibly finish during an ordinary workday?
5. How often do you think that you will not be able to satisfy the conflicting demands of various people around you?
6. How often do you feel that you are not fully qualified to handle your job?
7. How often do you know what your superior thinks of you, how he evaluates your performance?
8. How often do you find yourself unable to get information needed to carry out your job?

*Adapted from Kahn et al.[285]

9. How often do you worry about decisions that affect the lives of people that you know?
10. How often do you feel that you may not be liked and accepted by people at work?
11. How often do you feel unable to influence your immediate supervisor's decisions and actions that affect you?
12. How often do you not know just what the people you work with expect of you?
13. How often do you think that the amount of work you have to do may interfere with how well it is done?
14. How often do you feel that you have to do things on the job that are against your better judgment?
15. How often do you feel that your job interferes with your family life?

Each patient answered these 15 questions, resulting in a job stress score computed as follows: employees were asked to indicate on a five-point scale (0 = never, to 5 = nearly all the time) their feelings with relation to each question. The average of these items was then computed for each individual and these averages resulted in the job stress score. Those who scored in the upper range were grouped with patients who scored in the lower range as stress-related signs and symptoms appeared in both groups.

Weiman[288] showed that a disease/risk factor occurs more frequently when workers are either deprived of stimulation or are overloaded. His work confirmed Selye's[294] hypothesis, that deprivation as well as excess of stimuli is accompanied by an increase in stress. Therefore, employees with job stress scores greater than 2.5 (indicating overload) were grouped with employees whose scores were less than 1.3 (indicating deprivation of stimulation). The second group consisted of employees whose job stress scores fell in the middle range (indicating moderate job stress reactions).

The objectives of the project were to determine if intervention by interview would have any effect in reducing illness absentee rates; to provide information, educational materials and referral resources directed toward the reduction of stress-related symptoms; and to educate employees about the benefits of prevention as well as periodic medical examinations.

SCREENING CRITERIA

Employees were selected for the preventive interview based on a fit with one or more of these criteria:
1. Job stress scores in the high and low range (<1.3 and >2.5)
2. Multiple symptoms that appeared to be stress-related
3. History of frequent visits to the medical department
4. Expressed job-related or personal problems accompanied by symptoms that appeared to be stress-related

In an effort to screen employees who had identified job stress through the medical history procedure, the nurses and doctors in the medical department referred employees whose job stress scores indicated stimulus overload (>2.5) or stimulus deprivation (<1.3) or who fit one or more of the screening criteria. The interview was then scheduled for these employees as part of the periodic examination. Others referred included employees who revealed personal problems, such as family, marital, or sexual concerns; those who had concerns for their job security or career paths, and those who indicated financial problems (Table 17-1).

Twelve percent of the employees engaged in the interview had multiple symptoms that appeared to be stress-related, such as digestive complaints, frequent headaches, sleep disturbances, weight changes, anxiety, and fatigue. These symptoms, for the most part, were determined to be related to job stressors and/or personal stressors.

THE INTERVIEW

The outline of the interview is discussed in chapter 15. The interview was designed to identify the effects of job stressors on the individual employee. Severity of symptoms,

Table 17-1
Screening Results

Presenting Problem	No. of Employees Seen (%)
Job stress scores in high and low range (<1.3 and >2.5)	478 (47.8)
Personal stress (includes family, marital, and sexual problems)	270 (27.0)
Career problems	35 (3.5)
Financial problems	19 (1.9)
Multiple symptoms and multiple visits to the medical department	120 (12.0)
Obesity	78 (7.8)

the nature of the stressors and the employee's ability to cope with these stressors were evaluated. Physical, emotional, and cognitive needs were assessed as well as how successfully employees maintained a balance in their lives with regard to time for work, family, and self.

Knippel[295] demonstrated in his medical assessments that "basic survival issues" such as nutrition, exercise, sleep patterns, recognition factors, and environmental factors must be accounted for when evaluating levels of health. Levi[109] discussed the behaviors, both active and passive, that can determine stress reactions in the workplace. Inquiries about survival issues, work habits, attitudes toward superiors, and attendance were therefore included in the dialogue. Moss[296] pointed out how change, transition, and deteriorating support systems can increase vulnerability to illness. Thus items related to work and family pressures were also incorporated into the dialogue with life events and their effects on coping abilities from the Holmes and Rahe scale.[289]

Greiff and Munter[297] emphasized the importance of developing adequate coping skills in maintaining an appropriate balance with regard to time for work, family, and self. Since their work seemed relevant, questions relating to these issues were included.

REFERRALS

The findings during the interview prompted referrals to in-house and outside services such as counseling, weight control, smoking cessation and exercise programs, relaxation methods, and physician referrals (Table 17-2). Career planning and educational offerings were also made available to employees by the employer.

ASSESSMENT OF ABSENTEEISM

1. *Change in absentee rate*. Two measures of absentee rates were obtained: one 6-month span prior to the interview and one 6-month span after it. Results were compared with established absentee norms for all corporate employees during the same time intervals (Table 17-3).

2. *Matched groups*. Two experimental groups were formed with high-absentee subjects: one contained subjects with both high and low job stress scores (N = 96) and the second group contained subjects with job stress scores in the middle range (N = 50). Two groups were then selected from the company population as control groups. These subjects had not been interviewed but had had a periodic examination in the medical department during the same time period. Subjects in the control groups were matched to subjects in the experimental groups (high-absentee employees) by sex, job classification, time interval (seasons), and job stress score.

3. *Questionnaire*. Questionnaires were sent to employees with high-absentee rates 6 weeks after the interview to determine, by subjective reporting, if the interview had been helpful.

Table 17-2
Referral Distribution

Referral Resources*	Managers		Support Staff		Total (%)
	Male	*Female*	*Male*	*Female*	
Career planning (management only)	12	9	0	0	2.1
Educational and career planning (support staff)	0	0	30	15	4.5
Employee assistance	9	23	31	49	11.2
Consulting psychiatrist	5	2	3	8	1.8
Weight programs (internal and external)	14	25	20	31	9.0
Blood pressure program (internal)	4	2	3	5	1.4
Nutritional information, including diets	32	36	30	37	13.5
Exercise program material	90	102	78	90	36.0
Relaxation techniques, material	70	97	52	68	28.7
Physician referrals	15	20	15	14	6.4
Smoking cessation programs	8	13	51	20	9.2
No referral necessary	30	20	21	16	8.7
Stress management skills training	49	23	28	14	11.4

*Employees may be referred to more than one resource, depending on need.

Table 17-3
Absentee Norms

Job Category	Sex	Illness, Absence Norms (days)
Managers	M	2.25
	F	4.08
Support Staff	M	4.11
	F	6.83

Questionnaire

1. During the interview, were you able to determine the areas of your own health care that you need to attend to?

2. Since the interview have you given a higher priority to these aspects of your own health care?
   Yes ___ No ___ Somewhat ___
   Comment: _____

3. Have you been able to improve upon your own abilities to cope with job and/or personal stress since this evaluation?
   Yes ___ No ___ Somewhat ___
   Comment: _____

4. Do you think that this health evaluation service is helpful in learning how to prevent or reduce symptoms related to stress?
   Yes ___ No ___ Somewhat ___

5. Do you have suggestions to improve upon this evaluation?
   _____
   _____

6. Would you recommend this health evaluation to your fellow employees as helpful in managing their own health care?
   Yes ___ No ___ Somewhat ___
   Comment: _____

RESULTS

Absenteeism. Absentee rates for *all* employees interviewed were examined for the 6-month time period prior to their individual interview. This was done by code number to preserve anonymity.

Of the 1000 employees interviewed, 20.7% were found to have absentee rates above the norm for the 6-month period prior to the interview. This percentage was approximately the same across job classification and for men and women. Data on absentee rates are probably less reliable for management since the reporting system is not as well defined as it is for support staff; absentee rates for management are probably higher than statistics indicate.

In all three groupings of stress scores the experimental groups exhibited a decrease in average rate of absenteeism in the period following the interview in comparison with the period prior to the interview. Over the same 12-month period the control groups in all stress levels displayed an increase in the average number of days absent from the first 6-month period to the second 6-month period. The factors accounting for this phenomenon have not been determined although it is likely that a normal regression toward the mean would occur over a longer time period.

These data were then subjected to a regressed change analysis in which the effects of sex, job classification, and job stress score were eliminated prior to correlating the effects of the intervention and levels of absenteeism. This method allows a focus on the effects of the dialogue while controlling other possible contributing factors by holding them constant. When evaluated by a hierarchical regression analysis, the significance of the relationship between the interview process and absenteeism in the second 6-month period becomes apparent ($F = 6.261$ $P < .01$).

For those with high or low job stress scores ($<1.3, >2.5$), the experimental group decreased in average number of days absent from 5.078 in the 6 months prior to the dialogue to 2.922 in the 6 months after the dialogue. During the same time the control group increased in average number of days absent from 1.481 to 1.760.

For those who scored in the middle range of job stress the effects were greater. For the group that was exposed to the health evaluation interview, the average absentee rate decreased from 7.302 prior to the interview to 2.163 in the 6 months after the interview. During the same time period the average rate of absenteeism for the control group increased from 2.860 to 4.744 days.

For those who scored in the middle range, there are indications that stressors from outside the workplace were major factors and these were also explored during the interview.

DISCUSSION

Employees with high or low job stress scores identified primary work stressors as lack of recognition by superiors, role conflict (particularly with peers), deadlines, and job unsuitability. Employees in this category exhibited persistent physical symptoms such as irregular sleep patterns, fatigue, headaches, gastric upsets, and weight loss or gain. Appropriate referrals were made where indicated during the interview.

Follow-up was done by questionnaire 6 weeks after the interview (Table 17-4) to determine whether the interview and/or referral had been helpful. The results are shown in Table 17-4. Using the data obtained from the interview process and questionnaire, a career stress management seminar series was developed to provide employees with greater opportunities to assess their attitudes and behaviors related to effective stress management of both occupational and personal stressors.

Table 17-4
Questionnaire Results

85%	Expressed having been able, as a result of the interview, to determine areas of their health care that they had neglected (awareness factor).
78%	Stated that they did give a higher priority to these aspects of their health care after the interview (motivation factor).
77%	Stated that their coping abilities have improved in handling job and/or personal stress since the interview (success factor).
85%	Stated that the health evaluation interview was helpful in learning how to prevent or reduce symptoms related to stress (educational factor).
88%	Would recommend this evaluation to fellow employees as helpful in managing their own health care.
12%	Were critical of the interview and did not find it helpful.

SUMMARY AND CONCLUSIONS

The effect of a single interview with employees covering their life experiences, stresses, and problems of adjustment in reducing absenteeism is evident when compared to the absentee rates of employees who were not subjected to the interview.

CHAPTER 18

PERSPECTIVE AND PREVENTIVE STRATEGIES

STEWART WOLF

Any active life is more or less stressful, but life's stresses are not necessarily destructive. Indeed, the challenge they pose may open the door to one of life's greatest joys, savoring the satisfaction of achievement. Rather than focusing on attempts to minimize stress, therefore, it may be more profitable for a company to help cultivate their workers' sense of pride, worth, and commitment, qualities that tend to counteract the negative effects of stresses.

The close linkage of good morale with success is well known to college and professional athletic coaches. Winning over a more talented team is often accomplished through the extra effort that stems from high morale and a sense of devotion to the welfare of the team. Club owners have often learned to their sorrow that buying superior players may not gain a pennant if full and mutual commitment to superior team play is lacking.

To avoid costly waste, companies, no matter how large, need to make reasonable provisions for the more or less universal psychological and social needs of their employees as well as to take into account the great diversity of individual needs, aspirations, and vulnerabilities.[298]

Several years ago, in a study of workers and their families, a New York firm of management consultants categorized nine requirements ranging from supplying physical comforts, educational opportunities, opportunities for a variety of experiences, challenges for achievement, security of employment, cultivating identification with peer groups, a sense of participation and involvement with the company, a sense of personal dignity and importance, and the means for the relief of emotional tension.[299]

ENCOURAGING MOTIVATION AND MORALE

Among the human needs listed above, those that, when attended to, most clearly enhance productivity are those that contribute to self-esteem as well as to "team spirit." These qualities are, of course, affected by circumstances at home and in social life as well as at work.

Considerable frustration and disappointment at work can be tolerated if the home situation is secure, supportive, and satisfying. Conversely, a secure, supportive, and satisfying situation at work can often enable a person to tolerate a good deal of frustration, lack of appreciation, and disappointment in his family setting, but when both situations are insecure, trouble is likely.

The unions have attempted to promote psychological well-being among workers by diminishing work time and increasing pay. Although they have effected vast improvements in working conditions and protected the workers from a multitude of abuses, they have generally failed to focus on ways to increase satisfactions from the work itself. Indeed, satisfactions may have been reduced by the limitations placed on work hours and dispersal of responsibility for a product or a service, a prominent trend in industrial practice that is attributable in large measure to union classification of job types and to many employers' "assembly line" approach to efficient operation. We are not likely to return to the days when artisans worked long hours with pleasure and satisfaction, spurred by pride in workmanship as well as ambition to be selected for advancement. The Volvo Company, however, has attempted to increase the employees' sense of identification with its product by having teams of workers assemble an entire vehicle. Other firms offer stock options to employees to increase their sense of identification with the company. In Yugoslavia a unique form of modified capitalism has evolved in which the companies are actually owned by the employees who elect their own management.

Early in this century the workers in large American industries lived in company-owned houses and bought their supplies in company stores. While abuses resulting from the companies' power and influence led to a revulsion and ultimate abandonment of such paternalistic arrangements, nevertheless, on the positive side, access to such company-owned facilities provided a social focus, identification with a community, and a sense of belonging.

What might be called paternalistic industrial practices still exist in Japan and offer enlightening data. Matsumoto[300] describes the nature of the employer-employee relationship in large Japanese companies as one of a bilateral commitment. Being hired by a Japanese firm is like becoming a member of the family. Most employees are hired at a young age and remain with the same company throughout their working lives.

During the years when the popularity of foreign cars was eroding the profits of American manufacturers, absenteeism among assembly line workers was high and recalls for manufacturing defects were embarrassingly frequent. The morale needed to reverse those situations and reestablish the competitive position of American automobile manufacturers was stimulated only when there was a serious threat of collapse of the domestic industry. In this parlous situation, cooperation between unions and management emerged as their common cause became evident.

Although not undertaken jointly with unions, many American businesses and industries that employ large numbers of people had made efforts to cultivate a sense of community among workers by providing opportunities for recreation and fellowship even with involvement of their families. They often failed, however, to go beyond these general measures to understand the individual needs of their employees which make for productivity. To deal with these needs requires open communication between employer and employee, especially at the time of employment, job change, or promotion.

For many years companies approached the matter of employee health with the remedy of insurance, which is essentially recompense after the fact. Recently the concept of prevention has become more popular. The aim, in Page's words, is to maintain vertical health and avoid horizontal illness.[3] Successful prevention goes well beyond screening for early signs of illness. It requires an understanding of the person, his background, aspirations, and vulnerabilities.

This sort of information is not readily available from psychological testing devices or questionnaires. They may help by giving valuable suggestive leads, but ultimately face-to-face discussions are required to reach any real understanding of the person and his situation.

Failure to recognize and deal with the separate peculiarities and proclivities of individuals is inherent in the rules of employment and promotion for unions and companies alike. They are made to be impersonal with the expressed aim of avoiding bias. Thus individual differences in interest, motivation, appetite for hard work, and self-discipline are likely not to be taken into account in the interest of fair and uniform treatment. In large corporations the same supposed evenhandedness extends to the executives, and, when pronounced, it is marked by a high rate of turnover with the losses usually among the most gifted and desirable.

PROBLEMS OF ASSIGNMENT

Because of impersonal personnel policies, personnel officers may be unaware of individual preferences, attitudes, and vulnerabilities, especially when promotions or reassignments are being considered. A switch or promotion from one to another type of job, however reasonable it might seem to the supervisor, may simply not fit the individual. Everyone brings to a job not only his type and level of intelligence, his measurable aptitudes, but also his personality and behavioral characteristics, his aspirations, and his special way of looking at the world. The consequences of a poor fit may be troublesome or even disastrous to the person, the unit, or even the company. Page, who was at one time medical director of Standard Oil Company of New Jersey, wrote extensively on this problem that he referred to as the square peg in the round hole. His experiences led him to formulate the following law of employment, "Any gross misassignment will eventually produce medical symptoms."[3]

Page cited what he called the "non-obvious case" in which there is an appearance of smooth adaptation to a job with the individual himself not even realizing that he has been misassigned. Page reported his findings from a study of 100 misassigned employees of a large corporation, none of whom, on careful medical investigation, were found to have what are usually referred to as organic diseases. The ailing employees fell into two age groups, 25 to 30 and 40 to 55 years. They complained mainly of gastrointestinal (GI) symptoms, headache, sleeplessness, despondency, stiffness, backache, fatigue, and palpitations. Page emphasized the tendency of such neurotic manifestations to become fixed in the face of an unsatisfactory and unfulfilling work life. He found that early recognition of the problem and attention to working out a suitable assignment were usually effective in ameliorating or eliminating the symptoms and greatly decreasing what had been a serious problem of absenteeism.

As Page tells it;

> . . . if no one else happens to observe what is happening, this individual will continue to push himself blithely into the performance of tasks against which his entire inner being

rebels. Eventually this inner being or subconscious will strike back in the only way it knows how, by producing a symptom of illness to warn the misassigned that it is time to stop, look, and listen. The same habits of self-deception which he has acquired in order to stick to his job will enable him to shrug off the first minor symptoms of potential functional illness. Even if he receives constructive medical advice at this point, he may refuse to accept it or act upon it, assuming that these symptoms, like the symptoms of his boyhood illnesses, will in time just go away. If by this time he is fairly well advanced into his middle years, this creeping loss of health will be progressive and, when he is finally forced to recognize his true predicament, irreversible.[3]

From these observations of Page and others who have studied people in their workplace, it seems evident that psychologically and socially based symptoms are costly to the employer. A study of a large number of employees of the telephone company by Hinkle et al found that roughly 70% of the illnesses and disabilities were experienced by 30% of the employees and that those people who had the greatest number of minor illnesses, such as colds and headaches, were also the victims of the largest number of major illnesses, including gallstones, uterine myomas, heart attacks, and cancer. It was striking that those considered to have had the greatest difficulties of personality adaptation were precisely those who had the most minor and major illnesses resulting in loss of efficiency and time at work.

THE MARGINAL PRODUCER

In the corporate world, the company with few cash reserves may function well and compete effectively in the market unless and until adversity strikes, causing serious losses or an urgent need for cash. At such times many formerly productive and profitable companies have collapsed. Among a company's employees there are likely to be people who might be compared to marginal producers, not in terms of a shortage of liquid reserves, but in terms of deficient psychologic and social resources to enable them to cope successfully during difficult circumstances. Accidents and injuries, even minor ones, are likely to reveal the presence of these marginal producers when the consequences of the event seem out of all proportion to the physical damage.[301] The following examples show that the intrinsic quality of an event was only a precipitating factor in the serious disability that resulted and that the nature and extent of the disability depended more on the characteristics of the person.

A 33-year-old merchant seaman, somewhat effeminate and possessed of recurrent doubts about his masculinity, married. Despite considerable anxiety, especially about his sexual competence, he managed to maintain a fairly satisfactory relationship with his wife. While he was on duty on his ship, he fell across a belaying pin and injured his membranous urethra. Prompt medical attention included repair of the urethral injury and an apparently uneventful recovery followed. Nevertheless, the man was henceforth impotent for which he blamed the injury and he accordingly sued the shipping company. The litigation was long and the evidence confused. He eventually was paid several hundred dollars, but neither he nor the shipping company was satisfied because there was no adequate legal precedent to provide for liability in which a more or less innocuous incident set off a chain of destructive circumstances not directly attributable to the incident itself. It was as if an automobile parked on a hill had stood still, even though the driver neglected to set the emergency brake. The minor event of an innocent bystander leaning against the front fender was enough to shift the balance and start the automobile careening down the hill to inflict property damage and perhaps loss of life.

Another patient was a 35-year-old woman, the wife of an Air Force officer, who, while living on a military base, contracted an ordinary head cold. She telephoned the base surgeon who in turn phoned the pharmacist requesting that some "cold pills" be sent to the officer's wife. The pills were sent; she took them and went about preparing for a dinner party. Within a half-hour she noted extraordinary dryness of the mouth, mild palpitation, and giddiness but was not hampered seriously in the preparation of dinner. Suddenly a screaming ambulance stopped at the door. Before she knew what was happening, she was on a stretcher being rushed to the base hospital. When she arrived she was placed in bed and impaled on the needles of two intravenous infusions. The first explanation came from a nurse who said that she had accidentally been given a large overdose of atropine. She told her that another woman who had received the cold tablets was having convulsions in a room down the hall. She said that there was some question as to whether or not the other patient would survive the incident. Our patient did not have convulsions, but the following morning when the anxiety of the staff seemed to be subsiding, she found herself twitching and jerking uncontrollably. She was unable to do any kind of skilled work. She lost her appetite and could not sleep. These symptoms persisted despite reassurances that she had recovered from the episode of atropine poisoning. When she was finally discharged from the hospital, the diagnosis was psychoneurosis, conversion hysteria. She learned that the pharmacist who filled the prescription for the cold tablets had included ten times the prescribed amount of atropine and that the discovery of this mistake had been the reason for all the excitement. A lawyer recommended that she bring suit against the government. In rapid sequence, her husband lost his job at the base and was transferred to an undesirable assignment where there was no opportunity for advancement. He was later picked up drunk by civilian authorities and disciplined by his commander. He was finally moved to another and even less desirable station to which he refused to take along his wife. She, in turn, attempted to get a job in her former capacity as a court stenographer but was unable to manage the Stenotype because of adventitious movements. When her suit came to trial, an expert witness testified that her complaints could not have been produced by the pharmacodynamic properties of atropine. Accordingly, no compensation was allowed.

The patient had been the only child of a broken family. She had done well in school and had worked hard to obtain a coveted job as a court stenographer when she met the man whom she married. Her husband turned out to be an immature, dependent, and somewhat irresponsible person who was potentially alcoholic. Repeatedly, when he was in trouble with his superiors, his wife's diplomacy was able to rescue him from serious trouble. By virtue of the respect in which she was held by the various commanding officers, she and her husband were able to establish a relatively fragile and delicately balanced adjustment. When the patient was suddenly whisked away from the house in the ambulance, her husband became frightened and utterly dependent upon her. Since no doctor took the trouble to make a thorough examination, she in turn was alarmed about a possible lasting handicap from the overdose of atropine. It was if a gun had been cocked and ready for firing. The woman's hysterical illness was clearly precipitated by the alarming events surrounding the atropine overdosage although another similarly dramatic event might also have precipitated a decompensation of her adjustment. Where does the liability lie?

The situation of this and other comparable patients may be analogous to the economic plight of the marginal producer. Under favorable circumstances such a person may be able to operate satisfactorily, but he fails in an unfavorable environment or when accidents occur. The event that precipitated this patient's illness might have been easily met and adapted to by a less "marginal producer." On the other hand, this patient's personal and family calamity might have been avoided had there been proper communication and attention to her natural feeling of alarm.

Individuals with neurotic tendencies, including marginal producers, are sure to be found among any large group of employees. They will likely include some of the most gifted and dedicated. During World War II some of the ablest and most resourceful and reliable soldiers were found to have clinically manifest signs of psychoneurosis.[302] Therefore, while weeding out such people prior to employment may be possible, it may not be wise or profitable. To harvest the talents of such employees may require what at first seems unduly costly, namely the capability in the medical department to maintain open and constructive communication with employees.

Weider,[303] working with the employees of the Caterpillar Tractor Co, was able to show that efforts to identify and maintain individual communication with potentially neurotic patients and those susceptible to disorders frequently classified as psychosomatic or functional could reduce financial losses for the company. The investment in providing the necessary expert personnel and of allowing time for interviewing and testing was much less than the losses from absenteeism and frequent visits to sick calls. Other studies have confirmed the potential profitability of attention to the psychological and social problems of workers and especially the value of measures designed to strengthen motivation and engender loyalty and commitment to fellow workers and to the broad mission of the organization.

CHAPTER 19

EXPERIENCE WITH PREVENTIVE MEASURES

GUNNAR SEVELIUS

The emerging realization that human behavior is the major reason for the most common and costly medical problems has brought the concept of behavioral medicine into prominence. As a new medical specialty its task is to evaluate the efficacy of techniques and devices that may help achieve behavioral changes that are conducive to health.

Medical diseases rooted in human behavior may be preventable with the proper educational strategy. Many industries have utilized wellness messages of various sorts and there are commercially distributed programs that still require verification of either medical or economic efficacy. In some executive settings, enormously expensive health facilities have been created without any confirmation of their effectiveness.[304]

This chapter describes our experience with wellness education as it evolved at Lockheed Missiles and Space Co, Inc (LMSC), Sunnyvale, Calif, and presents the evidence which we feel indicates that the program is effective. In the beginning it was not a planned research program for that purpose, but because we had established a feedback system we could document habit changes in our population. Our experience with ways of communicating with employees may be helpful to others.

HABIT CHANGING TECHNIQUES

Booklets

Studies of compliance relative to control of elevated blood pressure done by SRI International, at LMSC in the mid-1970s revealed that compliance was closely related to convenience: a modification modality that required an employee to deviate more than 15 minutes from his daily routine was met with a high degree of compliance resistance. The study also demonstrated that patient involvement and self-responsibility play important parts in compliance. There was, for instance, poorer control of blood pressure in those people who deferred all responsibility for their medical care to their doctor and assumed none themselves. For a medical treatment to be maximally effective, patient participation supported by medical education had to be a part of the system. A great interest in getting involved exists but the practical problem of developing the right modes of transferring sufficient medical knowledge to laymen to enable them to participate had to be developed.

It was decided to try a new kind of medical educational booklet. This booklet, written on a specific subject in lay language, would educate the reader to an informational level close to that of his own physician, thereby making him a partner with his doctor. The booklets would be distributed, free of charge, very conveniently from display stands located throughout the industrial plant. It was found that employees picked up booklets when they were motivated to read them. At that time they were most receptive to the information and also to habit change. Some took the information to their families, and thereby created a home support system. It became typical for employees who had read a booklet and had found the message credible to become advocates for it and to recommend the booklets to others. Booklet information became common topics for discussion at lunch; advocates actually became watchdogs over co-workers' health habits. This high degree of health awareness in the plant led first to an employee-sponsored exercise facility in 1979, and eventually to a company-sponsored wellness program in 1983. It was all peer pressure at work.*

During recent years Americans have become health and fitness conscious as a result of the campaigns which have been promoted within the general population, but the accelerated habit change which took place in the LMSC population before 1983 was greatly influenced by the medical educational booklets. Between 1978 and 1983 LMSC employees had, on an individual basis, picked up more than 30,000 booklets addressing risk factors for heart attacks, ie, exercise, blood pressure, weight and cholesterol, smoking and stress. The wellness organization, which was established in January 1983, enhanced peer pressure further by large habit-change campaigns addressing the same subjects.

Campaigns

Campaigns require a leader and an organization. As an example, the wellness organization at LMSC is currently composed of an advisory board with representatives from the employee benefits department, the medical department, the employees' recreational department, the management organization, personnel development, and the employees' assistance program and public relations department. There are two part-time executives, one from the employees' recreational department and one from the medical department. The advisory board recommends different themes to be highlighted in campaigns throughout the year. The ex-

---

*In a comparison of two similar plants, the one in which the booklet program had been introduced had the better health record as reflected by group insurance costs being one third less than for the plant where the program was not introduced.

ecutives implement these themes with the help of expertise from inside or outside the company. Each theme requires a theme leader for its implementation. Most of the time the executives act as theme leaders. The goal is to put on three to four campaigns per year.

Smaller corporations do not require this elaborate organization or high degree of professionalism. The popularity and wide employee support that most wellness programs receive right from the beginning fire innovativeness and bring out enthusiastic leaders. A professional educational background, particularly in physical or medical education, can be helpful for the organizer. Visits by the leaders to other corporations with previous experience or to professional conferences can also be inspiring. For a wellness program to last beyond the first year's enthusiasm it is necessary to assign a budget of time and money to the leader. The LMSC budget for wellness is less than $2.00 per employee. Campaigns usually highlight a specific theme. Common themes are those related to heart attack risk factors, family life, and common medical or safety problems, eg, weight control, nutrition, exercise, smoking, alcohol, back care, etc.

Outside organizations specializing in the specific subjects are often helpful in organizing the campaigns, particularly the nonprofit, public service organizations such as the American Heart Association, the American Lung Association, the American Cancer Society, etc. The campaigns themselves consist of a concentrated effort to distribute a particular educational message, and to bringing this message to the attention of as many employees as possible. The campaign effort consists of distribution of booklets, posters, and flyers, mailings, lectures, or whatever resources are available. When the campaign is over people should not be left with just a slogan but with true insight into the reasons for and methods to control a behavioral problem.

Booklet information already present in the target population tends to enhance the campaign message. Employees thus

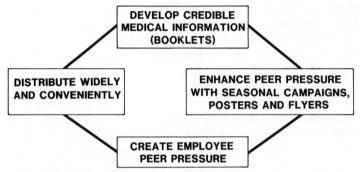

Figure 19-1 Successful health promotion techniques.

primed with knowledge become group leaders or advocates
of a campaign message. It is like having a promoter of the
campaign in each work station. The system can be likened
to a rolling snowball in that the demand for education just
grows and grows (Figure 19-1).

Some companies enhance campaigns with small incentives. Most of them have had success with T-shirts, certificates
of completion, or some recognition in the company publication. Very often employees themselves start some internal
wager system or contests.

Group Lectures

Lectures have the advantage of being very informative,
especially if delivered in person rather than taped. If the lec-
turer is well known he or she might draw a moderately large
audience (200 to 300). Lectures can be targeted to certain
populations depending on their specific needs. If the target
population is not too large lectures might be the best means
of relaying a message. If, however, the message has to be
given to a very large and widely dispersed population the
value of the lecture weakens. In general, lectures fit the needs

of comparatively small groups of "lecture-apt" people. In the LMSC weight loss program, for instance, lectures on behavior modification and nutrition were offered but were attended by less than 10% of the participating population. Analysis of the results revealed that attending lectures did not influence the resultant weight loss.[305]

The lack of effectiveness of wellness program lectures may be attributed to other disadvantages inherent in lectures. In most instances they are effective only when addressed to an audience of 30 to 40 people. They are inconvenient and time-consuming in that they require someone to break his daily routine to attend the lecture. If they are scheduled during working hours they are very costly. The timing of a lecture may or may not coincide with the receptiveness of many employees whose needs and commitments vary throughout the years.

Video Tapes

To economize on the cost of instructor fees (which is actually the least expensive cost item) some wellness programs use taped lectures. Presentations may be effective if offered during work hours. In our experience very few employees remain after work to attend a taped lecture on a wellness subject.

Executive Health Examinations

Regularly scheduled physical examinations have in recent years been criticized for lack of economic efficacy; it has been pointed out that few diseases are being discovered thanks to such examinations.[306] The main value of the executive physical examination, in our experience, has not been in the discovery of pathology but in benefits that have resulted from the opportunity of individual counseling.

The medical value of the executive examination is similar to that of a wellness program. It is an expensive mode of education but it is offered to the company's most valuable employees and it has been found to be effective as a stress or anxiety reliever.

Health Risk Appraisals

The health risk appraisal, like the executive examination, is a way of tailoring a wellness message to a specific individual. The employee is asked to complete a questionnaire regarding his own life-style habits; based on this information his life expectancy is compared to that of an individual who does not engage in the risky habits. The life expectancy for the subject is calculated according to a multiple regression formula in which each risk is weighed according to national statistics.

The Centers for Disease Control in Atlanta acts as a coordinator for health risk appraisal programs and has offered a model program for the price of the tape. Other programs are available commercially; some require analysis of the questionnaire by a main-frame computer and some by a personal computer; others use self-scoring.

The health risk appraisal in our experience enhances the wellness message because it deals with the specific problem of a particular individual although it offers little in the way of medical education or explanation. Standing alone, the health risk appraisal seems meager but when it is a part of a total wellness message it might be an effective component.

Employee Assistance Programs

Employee assistance programs (EAPs) direct themselves to help employees who are dependent on habits which relate to substance abuse. Employees may admit themselves to the

EAP or be directed by the company to participate in the program. When the employee has admitted himself voluntarily, his treatment is handled with utmost confidentiality.

When an employee's abuse of alcohol has come to the attention of the company because of poor performance, the employee may be fired, but may negotiate full reinstatement provided he rids himself of the abusive habit. The EAP counselor is responsible for following his progress. In either case, voluntary or nonvoluntary, the motivation to correct a poor habit is high within most EAP programs. Sustained abstinence for 3 years is about 70% in most programs. In an EAP designed like the one at LMSC, it can be expected that 0.25% of the employee population will need help from EAP each year.

For an employee assistance program to be successful it is important to have good root support in the employee population. To meet this need the EAP counselor at LMSC is part of an action committee consisting of Alcoholics Anonymous (AA) members/employees. An EAP program can spare valuable employees and their families stressful life events. Those who have successfully participated in this counseling, voluntarily or not, are always grateful.

Peer Support Systems

The concept of peer support, which has been successfully developed by AA, has been used with like success in other groups of chronic medical conditions, particularly those that influence people's total life style. There are now large nationally organized peer support groups for diabetes, heart disease, cancer, and neurologic and other diseases too numerous to publish here. Information about them can be obtained from county medical societies. To offer this service within the workplace will help many employees and their families to control stress from life events.

Insurance Incentives

Everyone was at equal risk to become sick in the past when most diseases were of an infectious nature. It was then fair for the majority to help pay for medical treatment for the minority who actually became sick. At present we are all not at the same risk for illness. As stated earlier many current diseases are rooted in poor health habits. Some diseases are actually due to injuries that people, with full knowledge of the consequences, inflict on their bodies. One might now question the fairness of asking the majority to pay the medical bills for self-inflicted medical conditions. Financial incentives are effective in directing people's behavior in many areas of life. It seems good business management to include some financial incentives in insurance coverage to encourage the maintenance of sound health habits.

Feedback Systems

To document the effect of educational programs it is necessary to have a feedback system to monitor the habits of the target population. Because employers must normally ignore personal information not relevant to work, company-initiated studies must be anonymous and hence will not reveal unhealthy habits of specific individuals.

The handicap is avoided at LMSC by having surveys performed by independent outside agencies. Questionnaires concerning changes may be sent to the total employee population or to a randomized sample, before and after a habit-changing intervention. It is important to verify that the sample returned represents the total target population.

RESULTS

The first evidence that our medical education efforts might be effective was revealed in two blood pressure surveys.

The first survey, which covered a random selection of 3000 employees, revealed a prevalence of elevated arterial pressure in 17%.

Subsequently the company distributed about 30,000 educational booklets addressing risk factors in hypertension and heart attacks. Following that a second blood pressure survey was made which included 7200 employees. Elevated blood pressure in both surveys was established by three separate recordings. The second survey revealed elevated blood pressure in only 1.7% of the employees,[307] a striking decrease from 17%.

Paralleling these findings the medical department recorded a drop of 80% in time lost due to high blood pressure. Perhaps most striking is the fact that the blood pressure of these employees has essentially stayed down since then. The change in high blood pressure cannot be attributed only to our in-house educational efforts. There was at the same time a nationwide health educational program to control high blood pressure. Irrespective of the source of the health education, however, the findings strongly support its efficacy.

Even more impressive were the results of the study done on the 1.7% of the population that still had high blood pressure. They were divided into two treatment groups and a control group. The treatment groups were exposed to different nonpharmaceutical interventions, namely biofeedback and progressive relaxation.

Blood pressure improved in both of the treatment groups. Within 4 months blood pressure was close to normal and stayed down for a 3-year observation period. Surprisingly, the blood pressures of the control group were also lowered following the self-administered health education experience.

LIFE-STYLE SURVEY

In order to establish, company-wide, a data base of the current health habits of the employee population that could serve as a base line for evaluating the efficacy of future educational programs, a health habit questionnaire was sent to 23,000 employees; more than 9000 were returned (Figure 19-2).

The sample was found to be representative of the rest of the LMSC population with respect to known variables such as sex, age, and seniority.

Smoking

The prevalence of smoking, according to sex and age, is shown in Figure 19-3. Females now constitute, as a percentage, the majority of smokers. Nationally, 34% of the population smoke; at LMSC only 17% of the population smoke and of the 83% of nonsmokers, 41% had been smokers but quit successfully following our antismoking booklet campaign. This is surprising in view of the fact that smoking is said to be one of the most difficult habits to give up. The reduction in smoking among employees has not as yet altered the working time lost to pulmonary diseases. About 1000 days per 1000 employees have been saved since 1978 without any definite trend toward decrease as yet (Figure 19-3).

Exercise

The answers to the exercise question indicated that almost 60% of employees exercise regularly two or three times per week. Less than 10% use the company's exercise facility, apparently preferring to exercise on their own time. Those who do use the company facility seem to be very committed to an exercise routine.

Stress

One of the most interesting findings in the answers to the question on stress was that in all age groups, women felt more

LMSC LIFE-STYLE SURVEY

The purpose of this confidential survey is to provide information for planning Wellness Program activities. Please take a few minutes to complete the questions on the reverse side. Do not sign your name. Any additional comments are appreciated. Thank you for your time and effort.

Linda Seidman
Linda Seidman
Wellness Program Chairman

G. Sevellius M.D.
Dr. Gunnar Sevellius
Medical Director

Comments: _____

_____

_____

_____

_____

Please return by July 29, 1983, to: Wellness Program, Orgn. 27-34, Bldg. 106, Fac. 1.

(OVER)

Figure 19-2 Questionnaire for life-style survey.

LMSC LIFE-STYLE SURVEY

INSTRUCTIONS: Mark the box that best describes you.

My sex is: Male ☐   Female ☐

My current marital status is: Single ☐

Married	☐ How long? _____ /yrs
Separated	☐ How long? _____ /yrs
Divorced	☐ How long? _____ /yrs
Widowed	☐ How long? _____ /yrs

My age is: Under 25 ☐   25-34 ☐   35-44 ☐   45-54 ☐   55-64 ☐   65 and over ☐

I have worked for LMSC: Less than one year ☐
One to five years ☐
Five to ten years ☐
More than ten years ☐

	YES	NO
1. Do you exercise regularly (at least 15-20 minutes, 2-3 times a week)?	☐	☐
2. Do you smoke cigarettes daily?	☐	☐
3. Did you ever smoke cigarettes?	☐	☐
4. Are you more than 10 pounds overweight?	☐	☐
5. Do you feel excessive stress from:		
(a) Your marriage or relationship?	☐	☐
(b) Your children?	☐	☐
(c) Your financial situation?	☐	☐
(d) Your work situation?	☐	☐
6. Do you have time for relaxation or hobbies?	☐	☐
7. If you drink alcohol, how much:		
(a) Glasses of wine per week? _____ glasses		
(b) Bottles of beer per week? _____ bottles		
(c) Mixed drinks or shots of liquor per week? _____ drinks/shots		

Figure 19-2 *(continued)*

203

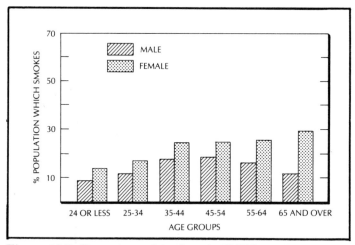

Figure 19-3 Percentage of smokers in LMSC population by sex and age, 1983 estimates.

stressed than men. Work stress was prominent in both sexes as were marriage stress, financial stress, and stress from teenaged children. The high stress noted in the post-65-year-old female group might not be significant due to the small sample size (Figures 19-4–19-7).

Alcohol

The responses to the questions on drinking habits confirmed the popular notion that beer is a young man's drink, wine, a woman's drink, and hard liquor, the older generations' drink. Sully* has considered the intake of more than 32 units

---

*"Sully" is A.J. Sullivan, executive engineer at Standard Oil of California. He successfully recovered from alcoholism 22 years ago and has since dedicated his life to working with more than 4000 affected people. Sully was one of the 11 founders and the second president of ALMACA (Association of Labor, Management, and Consultants on Alcoholism).

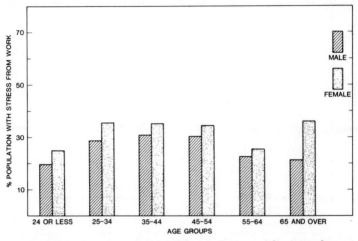

Figure 19-4 Percentage of LMSC population with stress from work by sex and age, 1983 estimates.

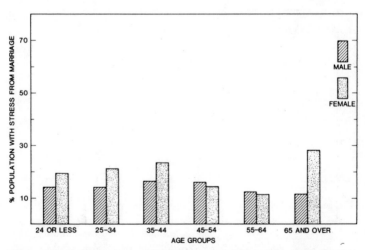

Figure 19-5 Percentage of LMSC population with stress from marriage by sex and age, 1983 estimates.

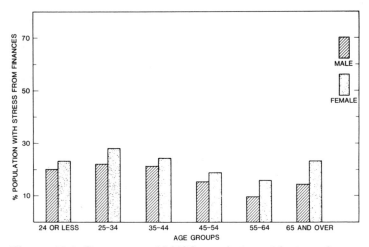

Figure 19-6 Percentage of LMSC population with stress from fiances by sex and age, 1983 estimates.

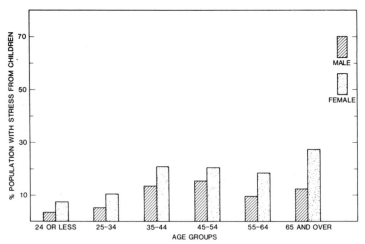

Figure 19-7 Percentage of LMSC population with stress from children by sex and age, 1983 estimates.

Table 19-1
Distribution of Alcohol Consumption in
Lockheed (LMSC) Population

Drinks (wk)	Male	Female	Total
0	23%	31%	25%
1–14	57%	61%	58%
15–21	10%	5%	9%
22–31	6%	2%	5%
≥ 32	4%	1%	4%

of alcohol (bottles of beer, glasses of wine, ounces of liquor per week) to a high risk for self-destructive alcohol abuse. About 7% percent of these or slightly less than 0.25% of the entire employee population is admitted voluntarily or involuntarily to the EAP each year (Table 19-1).

Backache

Backache by itself may not be a stress disease but the lost time attributed to backache is closely related to stress. A supportive attitude by a company leads to a reduction of stress and a decrease in lost time. This is illustrated by the impact on lost time from occupational injury that a simple policy change made at LMSC. In 1978 LMSC implemented a Return to Work Committee with representation from the medical, labor relations, and workers' compensation departments, and affected employee supervisors. The purpose of the committee is to help an injured worker return to work as early as possible after a lost-time work injury, 40% of which are back injuries. Since the implementation of this committee there has been a steady, yearly decrease in lost time from the back as well as other injuries; the rate of lost time from occupational injury has decreased more than 50% over the last 5 years (Figure 19-8).

208

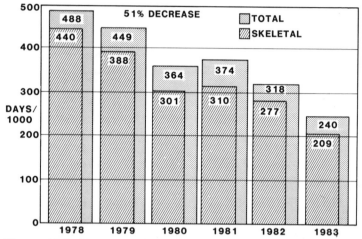

Figure 19-8 Occupational lost days per 1000: 1978–1983.

Weight

The answers to the weight question showed that about 60% of employees felt, in agreement with most other surveys, that they were at least 10 lb overweight.

A 3-month weight loss campaign was implemented in January 1983. It consisted of weigh-in and weigh-out records, self-educational materials, nutrition fairs, and lectures presented by taped and live instructors. Slightly more than 12% of the total population, 2500 persons, signed up. Of these, 1761 (70%) completed the program. Average weight loss was 8.3 lb, a total weight loss of 14,584 lb, or more than 7 tons! The cost of the campaign, including much of an expensive statistical analysis, was $5.00 per lb. Without this scientific analysis of the results it would probably have been possible to implement the campaign for half this amount.

Costs

The cost of the entire 1984 wellness campaign effort amounted to $2.00 per employee or 0.2% of the cost of group insurance.

The American Hospital Association estimated the hospital costs for smokers v nonsmokers and for those with normal v elevated blood pressure. The cost and possible cost savings when such figures are applied to the LMSC population are listed in Table 19-2.

The savings tend to go to the insurer in prepaid plans and to the employer only when he is self-insured. The cost per employee of self-administered indemnity plans has increased in California in recent years at an annual rate of 18%. At LMSC it has been possible to keep this rate down to 12% for the last 3 years, possibly reflecting a 6% decrease in utilization.

Although valid information on costs for specific diseases within corporations and insurance companies is essential to the validation of the medical and economic efficacy of any preventive health program, the data are very difficult to generate. However, the health education model used at LMSC involves so little cost that it seems reasonable to assume its economic efficacy in view of its demonstrated medical efficacy.

SUMMARY

Many of the most common, costly, and catastrophic illnesses are caused by our lifelong habits. Medical education can effect a change in these habits and therefore become important for the prevention of such diseases.

Different modes of education, such as booklets, campaigns, book/campaigns, lectures, tapes, managerial examinations, employee assistance programs, peer groups, financial incentives, and return to work committees, can be more or less ef-

Table 19-2
Estimation of Hospital Costs: Smoking v Nonsmoking;
Hypertension v Normal BP

Medical Trend	Excess Annual Medical Cost per Employee*	Incidence Before Education	After	Cost/1000 Employees Before Education	After	Savings/1000 Employees
Smoking	$400.00	36%	17.0%	$144,000	$68,000	$76,000
Hypertension	$275.00	17%	1.7%	$46,750	$ 4,675	$42,075
					Total	$118,075
					Educational costs	− 2,500
					Net Total	$115,575

*American Hospital Association estimates.

fective separately or collectively in accomplishing habit change.

This chapter, which has reviewed an experience with health education at Lockheed Missiles and Space Co, has shown that poor health habits can be changed with surprisingly simple and inexpensive educational packages. The industrial setting thus appears altogether suitable for such programs.

AFTERWORD

This book has been directed mainly to those whose responsibilities include the health of employees, chiefly physicians, other health professionals, supervisory and management personnel. The aim has been to provide useful information and understanding of occupational stress from a variety of different viewpoints including those of researchers, industrial consultants, medical school faculty, and medical directors of corporations.

The authors representing these viewpoints have provided evidence from controlled observations and experiments as well as surveys and case studies. They have not dealt with the tangible hazards of the work place, such as potential exposure to injury or toxic chemicals. These important aspects of occupational health have been well covered in other excellent publications. Instead, they have tried to correct what has been insufficient awareness of social and emotional problems that may also be hazardous to the health and productivity of workers. On the other hand, they have emphasized the salubrious effects of high group morale and of individual job satisfaction, a sense of accomplishment, and a feeling of being recognized and appreciated. Such constructive social and psychological forces may even mitigate the effects of exposure to physical and chemical risks.[308]

Although at any one time an estimated 8% to 10% of the national workforce are experiencing disabling stress-related symptoms,[309] the psychologic and social factors do not act alone or in isolation. They are part of an interacting complex of factors that determine one's level of health and well being.

Since an analysis of the significance of occupational stresses requires an understanding of individual peculiarities, motivations and vulnerabilities, it follows that the more one knows about the worker as a person, the more effectively he can be adapted to his job.

Successful treatment of employees with stress-related disorders may at times require individual or group therapy and at other times only encouragement and efforts to bolster coping mechanisms. When coping involves reliance on alcohol and other mood-altering drugs, however, more formally organized efforts are required as provided by employee assistance programs.

The responsibilities and liabilities of employers and their corporate medical departments have been outlined. Treatment strategies have been considered and some existing programs directed toward educating workers and preventing stress-related disorders have been described.

Not only must business and industry-related medical facilities be concerned with the health effects of occupational stress but so must physicians and other health care personnel who deal with patients away from the workplace. The important area of the education of physicians, nurses, and others in the broad field of occupational stress will require, therefore, new emphasis and continuing attention. We hope that this volume will appeal to students of medicine and other health professionals and that to some extent it may fill gaps in their formal academic curricula. Increasing reliance on burgeoning medical technology and restriction of interest to ever narrowing specialities must be balanced by learning experiences that promote an appreciation of the uniqueness of the person and of his or her responses, either salutary or unhealthy, to surrounding circumstances at home or at work.[310]

Stewart Wolf
Albert J. Finestone

BIBLIOGRAPHY

1. Robertson RB Sr: Opening Remarks. A report of the Third Annual Lake Logan (NC) Conference, May 1957.
2. Mather C: *Angel of Bethesda.* Boston, Beall & Shryock, 1954.
3. Page RC: *Occupational Health and Mantalent Development.* Berwyn, Ill, Physicians' Record Company, 1963.
4. Wolf S, Bruhn JG, Goodell H: *Occupational Health as Human Ecology.* Springfield, Ill, Charles C Thomas Publisher, 1978.
5. Osler W: *The Principles and Practice of Medicine,* ed 5. New York and London, Appleton-Century-Crofts, 1903.
6. Wolf S: Psychosocial forces in myocardial infarction and sudden death. *Circulation Suppl* 1969;5:74–83.
7. Hinkle LE, Redmont R, Plummer N, et al: An examination of the relation between symptoms, disability and serious illness in two homogeneous groups of men and women. *Am J Public Health* 1960;50:1327.
8. Wolff HG: *Stress and Disease.* Springfield, Ill, Charles C Thomas Publisher, 1952.
9. Wolf S, Goodell H: *Stress and Disease,* ed 2. Springfield, Ill, Charles C Thomas Publisher, 1968.
10. Levi L: *Society, Stress and Disease.* New York, Oxford University Press, 1971.
11. Cannon WB: *Bodily Changes in Pain, Hunger, Fear and Rage.* New York, Appleton-Century-Crofts, 1929.
12. Wolf S, Wolff HG: *Human Gastric Function: An Experimental Study of a Man and His Stomach,* ed 2. New York, Oxford University Press, 1947.
13. Wolff HG: *Change in Vulnerability of Tissue: An Aspect of Man's Response to Threat.* The National Institute of Health Annual Lectures, US Department of Health, Education and Welfare, Publication No 388, 1953, pp 38–71.
14. Thoreau HD: *Walden: A Writer's Edition.* New York, Holt, Rinehart & Winston Inc, 1961.
15. Hershey P, Blanchard KH: *Management of Organizational Behavior Utilizing Human Resources,* ed 2. Englewood Cliffs, NJ, Prentice-Hall, 1977.

216

16. Whyte WH Jr: *The Organization of Man.* New York, Double-day & Co, 1956.
17. Hippocrates: *Works of Hippocrates: Medical Classics.* Baltimore, Williams & Wilkins Co, 1938, vol 3.
18. Ramazzini B: *Translation of the Latin text of De Morbis Artificum Diatriba of 1713,* translation published under the auspices of the NY Academy of Medicine, New York, Hafner Press, 1964.
19. Cabanis JPG: *On the Relations between the Physical and Moral Aspects of Man,* Mora G, Saidi MD (eds). Baltimore, The Johns Hopkins University Press, 1981.
20. Locke J: *An Essay Concerning Human Understanding, in 4 Books.* London, Elizabeth Hold, 1690.
21. Gassendi P: *Institutio logica, et philosophiae epicuri syntagma.* London, R Daniel, 1660.
22. Thackrah CT: *The Effects of the Principal Arts, Trades and Professions and of Civic States and Habits of Living on Health and Longevity.* Philadelphia, Porter, 1831.
23. Oliver T (ed): *Dangerous Trades: The Historical, Social and Legal Aspects of Industrial Occupations as Affecting Health by a Number of Experts.* London, John Murray, 1902.
24. Oliver T: *Diseases of Occupation From The Legislative, Social and Medical Points of View.* London, Methuen & Co, 1908.
25. Hill LE: *Caisson Sickness and the Physiology of Work in Compressed Air.* London, E Arnold, 1912.
26. Kober GM: *Industrial and Personal Hygiene. A Report of the Committee on Social Betterment.* Washington, President's Homes Committee, 1908.
27. Mock HE: Industrial medicine and surgery: The new specialty. *JAMA* 1917;68:1–11.
28. Hamilton A: *Report on Industrial Poisons.* Washington, Government Printing Office, Bureau of Labor Bulletin No. 95, 1911.
29. Munsterberg H: *Psychology and Industrial Efficiency.* New York, Houghton-Mifflin Co, 1913.
30. Viteles MS: *Industrial Psychology.* London, Jonathan Cape, 1933.
31. Viteles MS: *Motivation and Morale in Industry.* New York, WW Norton & Co, 1953.
32. Hoffman FL: Industrial Accident Statistics. US Bureau of Labor Statistics Bull No. 157. Washington, Government Printing Office, 1915.
33. Rothlistberger FJ, Dickson WJ: *Management and the Worker: An Account of a Research Program Conducted by the Western*

Electric Co, Hawthorne Works, Chicago. Cambridge, Harvard University Press, 1939.

34. Gregg A, in *Harvard Medical Alumni Bulletin.* Cambridge, Harvard University Press, 1936.

35. Wiener N: *Cybernetics, or Control and Communication In The Animal and The Machine.* New York, John Wiley & Sons, 1948.

36. McCulloch W: Introductory discussion, in Von Foerster H (ed): *Cybernetics.* New York, Josiah Macy Jr Foundation, 1950.

37. Wolf S: *Social Environment and Health.* Jessie and John Danz Lecture, Seattle, Washington, 1980.

38. Ross WD: *Practical Psychiatry for Industrial Physicians.* Springfield, Ill, Charles C Thomas Publisher, 1956.

39. Major RH: *A History of Medicine.* Springfield, Ill, Charles C Thomas Publisher, 1954, vol 4, p 1021.

40. Camus A: *The Plague,* Gilbert S (trans). New York, Alfred A Knopf Inc, 1948.

41. Richardson EL: in forward to *Work in America.* A report of a special task force to the Secretary of HEW, prepared under the auspices of the WE Upjohn Institute for Employment Research. Cambridge, MIT Press, 1973.

42. Taylor FW: *Principles of Scientific Management.* New York, Harper & Bros, 1911.

43. Benet S: *Abkhasians: The Long Living People of the Caucasus.* New York, Holt, Rinehart & Winston, 1965.

44. Bruhn JG, Wolf S: *The Roseto Story: An Anatomy of Health.* Norman, Oklahoma, University of Oklahoma Press, 1978.

45. Report of the Special Task Force to Secretary of HEW. Washington, Government Printing Office, 1973.

46. Kobassa SC, Maddi SR, Covington S: Personality and constitution as mediators in the stress-illness relationship. *J Health Soc Behav* 1981;22:367–378.

47. Wolf S, Wolff HG: *Human Gastric Function: An Experimental Study of Man and His Stomach,* ed 2. New York, Oxford University Press, 1947.

48. Manning GW: Symposium–Central integration of cardiovascular control: A distributed neural network. *Fed Proc* 1980;39: 2485–2530.

49. Hoff EC, Greene CW: Cardiovascular reactions induced by electrical stimulation of the cerebral cortex. *Am J Physiol* 1936; 117:411.

50. Denny-Brown D, Robertson EG: On the physiology of micturition. *Brain* 1933;56:149.

51. Lapides J: Function of skeletal muscle in control of urination. 2: Effect of complete skeletal muscle paralysis. *Surg Forum* 1956;6:613.
52. Gaskell WH: On the structure, distribution and function of the nerves which innervate the visceral and vascular systems. *J Physiol* 1885;7:1–80.
53. Langley JN, Anderson KK: The constituents of hypogastric nerves. *J Physiol* 1894;17:177–190.
54. Eppinger H, Hess L: *Vagotonie; klinische Studie.* Berlin, A Hirschwald, 1910.
55. Danilewski B: Experimentelle Beiträge zur Physiologie des Gehirns. *Pflugers Arch Ges Physiol* 1875;11:128–138.
56. Karplus JP, Kreidl A: Ein Sympathicuszentrum im Zwischenhirn. *Arch Ges Physiol* 1910;135:401–416.
57. Gunn CG, Sevelius G, Puggari MJ, et al: Vagal cardiomotor mechanisms in the hind brain of the dog and cat. *Am J Physiol* 1968;214:258–262.
58. Wolf S: Psychophysiological influences on the dive reflex in man, in Schwartz P, Brown AM, Melliani A, et al (eds): *Neural Mechanisms in Cardiac Arrhythmias.* New York, Raven Press, 1978, pp 237–250.
59. Grace WJ, Graham DT: The specificity of the relation between attitudes and disease. *Psychosom Med* 1952;14:243.
60. Cousins N: *Anatomy of an Illness.* New York, WW Norton & Co, 1979.
61. Cousins N: Anatomy as an illness (as perceived by the patient). *N Engl J Med* 1976;295:1458–1463.
62. Cousins N: *The Healing Heart, Antidotes to Panic and Helplessness.* New York, WW Norton & Co, 1983.
63. Bean WB: *Sir William Osler Aphorisms.* Springfield, Ill, Charles C Thomas Publisher, 1951, p 97.
64. Cannon WB, de la Paz D: Emotional secretion of adrenal secretion. *Am J Physiol* 1911;28:64–70.
65. Dale HH: On the action of ergotoxine; with special reference to the existence of sympathetic vasodilation. *J Physiol* 1913;46:291–300.
66. Ahlquist RP: A study of the adrenotropic receptors. *Am J Physiol* 1948;153:586–599.
67. Cryer PE: Catecholamines and metabolism introduction. *Am J Physiol* 1984;10:E1–3.
68. Bahnsen M, Burrin JM, Johnston DG, et al: Mechanism of catecholamine effects on ketogenesis. *Am J Physiol* 1984;10:E173–179.

69. Lefkowitz RJ: Direct binding studies of adrenergic receptors: Biochemical, physiologic and clinical implications. *Ann Intern Med* 1979;91:450–458.

70. Cryer PE, Santiago JV, Shah S: Measurement of norepinephrine and epinephrine in small volumes of human plasma by a single isotope derivative method: Response to the upright posture. *J Clin Endocrinol Metab* 1974;39:1025–1029.

71. Garber AJ, Cryer PE, Santiago JV, et al: The role of adrenergic mechanisms in the substrate and hormonal response to insulin-induced hypoglycemia in man. *J Clin Invest* 1976;58:7–15.

72. Brown MR, Fisher LA: Brain peptides as intercellular messengers. *JAMA* 1984;251:1310–1315.

73. Axelrod J, Reisine TD: Stress hormones: Their interaction of regulation. *Science* 1984;224:452–459.

74. Snyder SH: Drug and neurotransmitter receptors in the brain. *Science* 1984;224:22–31.

75. Beaumont W: *Experiments and Observations in the Gastric Juice and the Physiology of Digestion.* Plattsburg, F.P. Allen, 1833.

76. Wolf S: Effects of suggestion and conditioning of the action of chemical agents in human subjects. *J Clin Invest* 1950;20:100.

77. Chey WY: *Functional Disorders of the Digestive Tract.* New York, Raven Press, 1983.

78. Kottke FJ, Kubicek WG, Visscher MB: Production of arterial hypertension by chronic renal artery nerve stimulation. *Am J Physiol* 1945;145:38–47.

79. Frohlich ED, Pfeffer MA: Adrenergic mechanisms in human hypertension and in spontaneously hypertensive rats. *Clin Sci Mol Med* 1975;48:225–238.

80. Arnetz BB, Theorell T, Levi L, et al: An experimental study of the social isolation of elderly people: Psychoendocrine and metabolic effects. *Psychosom Med* 1983;45:395–406.

81. Volpe R: The role of auto-immunity in hypoendocrine and hyperendocrine function with special emphasis on auto-immune thyroid disease. *Ann Intern Med* 1977;87:86–99.

82. Stein M, Schiavi RC, Camerino M: Influence of brain and behavior on the immune system. *Science* 1976;191:434–440.

83. Emotions and immunity, editorial. *Lancet,* July 20, 1985.

84. Borysenko M, Borysenko J: Stress, behavior and immunity: Animal models and mediating mechanisms. *Gen Hosp Psychiatry* 1982;4:59–67.

85. Locke SE: Stress, adaptation and immunity: Studies in humans. *Gen Hosp Psychiatry* 1982;4:58–59.

86. Hinkle LE Jr: *The Effect Of Exposure To Culture Change, Social*

Change and Changes in Interpersonal Relationships on Health.
New York, John Wiley & Sons, 1974.
87. Bockus HL (ed): *Gastroenterology.* Philadelphia, WB Saunders Co, 1976.
88. Ratcliff HL, Cronin MTI: Changing frequency of atherosclerosis in mammals and birds in the Philadelphia Zoological Gardens. *Circulation* 1958;18:41–52.
89. Kaplan JR, Manuck SB, Clarkson TB: Social status, environmental and atherosclerosis in cynomologous monkeys. *Arteriosclerosis* 1982;2:356–358.
90. Groen JJ, Tijong BK, Willebrandt AF, et al: *Influence of nutrition, individuality and different forms of stress on blood cholesterol.* Results of an experiment of 9 months duration in 60 normal volunteers. Proceedings of the First International Congress of Dietetics. Volding (10), 1959.
91. Groover ME Jr: Clinical evaluation of a public health program to prevent coronary artery disease. *Trans Coll Phys* 1957;24:105.
92. Grundy SM, Griffin AC: Effects of periodic mental stress on serum cholesterol levels. *Circulation* 1959;19:496.
93. Cathey C, Jones HB, Naughton J, et al: The relationship of life stress to concentration of serum lipids in patients with coronary artery disease. *Am J Med* 1962;244:421–441.
94. Wolf S, McCabe WR, Yamamoto J, et al: Changes in serum lipids in relation to emotional stress during rigid control of diet and exercise. *Circulation* 1962;26:379–387.
95. Leriche R, Fontaine R, Kunlin J: Contribution à l'étude des vasomoteurs coronaires. *CR Soc Biol (Paris)* 1932;110:299.
96. Hochrein M, Seggel KA: Uber den atpischen Verlauf des Myokardinfarktes. *AF Klin Medizin,* Bd 125: MIT 2 Textabildungen Eingegangen Am, 21 Mai, 1933, pp 161–174.
97. Rosenmann RH, Friedman M, Strauss R, et al: A predictive study of coronary heart disease. *JAMA* 1964;189:15–22.
98. Von Dusch T: *Lehrbuch der Herzkrankheiten.* Leipzig, Verlag von Wilhelm Engelman, 1868.
99. Osler W: The Lumleian lectures on angina pectoris. *Lancet* 1910;1:839–844.
100. Wolf SG, in Lewis H, Griswold H, Underwood H (eds): *Stress and Heart Disease. Modern Concepts of Cardiovascular Disease.* New York, American Heart Association, 1960, 29:559–603.
101. Wolf S, Cardon PV Jr, Shepard EM, et al: *Life Stress and Essential Hypertension.* Baltimore, Williams & Wilkins Co, 1955.
102. Bacon SD: Industry, the public and alcoholism. *Quart J Stud Alcohol* 1953;14:247.

103. Dunbar HF: *Psychosomatic Diagnosis.* New York, Hoeber & Harper, 1943.
104. Kagan AR, Levi L: Health and environment—psychosocial stimuli. A review. *Soc Sci Med* 1974;8:225–241.
105. Levi L, Andersson L: *Psychosocial Stress—Population, Environment and Quality of Life.* New York, Toronto, London, Sidney, Spectrum Publications, 1975.
106. Zenz C: *Occupational Medicine.* Chicago, Year Book Medical Publishers, 1975, pp 272–273.
107. Levi L: *Preventing Work Stress.* Reading, Mass, Addison-Wesley, 1981.
108. Levi L: Stress and distress in response to psychosocial stimuli. *Acta Med Scand (Suppl)* 1972;191:528.
109. Levi L (ed): *Society, Stress & Disease: Working Life.* Oxford, New York, Toronto, Oxford University Press, 1981, vol 9.
110. Frankenhaeuser M: The role of peripheral catecholamines in adaptation to understimulation and overstimulation, in Serban G (ed): *Psychopathology of Human Adaptation.* New York, Plenum Press, 1976, pp 173–191.
111. Frankenhaeuser M: Coping with job stress—a psychobiological approach, in Gardell G, Johansson G (eds): *Working Life. A Social Science Contribution to Work Reform.* London, John Wiley & Sons, 1981.
112. Frankenhaeuser M, Johansson G: Task demand as reflected in catecholamine excretion and heart rate. *J Human Stress* 1976;2:15–23.
113. Frankenhaeuser M, Gardell B: Underload and overload in working life: Outline of a multidisciplinary approach. *J Human Stress* 1976;2:35–46.
114. Johansson G, Aronsson G, Lindstrom BO: Social psychological and neuroendocrine stress reactions in highly mechanized work. *Ergonomics* 1978;21:583–599.
115. Gardell B: *Psychosocial Aspects of Industrial Production Methods.* Reports from the Department of Psychology, University of Stockholm, 1979, suppl 47.
116. Gardell B: *Scandinavian research on stress in working life.* Read before IRRA Symposium on Stress in Working Life. Denver, Colo, September 5–7, 1980.
117. Ahlbom A, Karasek R, Theorell T: Psykosociala arbetskrav och risk for hjart-karldod. (Psychosocial occupational demands and risk for cardiovascular death.) *Lakartidningen* 1977;77: 4243–5245.
118. Karasek R: Job demands, job decision latitude and mental

strain: Implications for job re-design. *Administrative Science Q* 1979;24:285–308.

119. Karasek R: Job socialization and job strain. The implications of two related psychosocial mechanisms for job design, in Gardell B, Johansson G (eds): *Working Life. A Social Science Contribution to Work Reform.* London, John Wiley & Sons, 1981.

120. Gardell B: *Arbetsinnehall och Livskalitet.* (Job Content and Quality of Life.) Stockholm, Prisma, 1976.

121. Wilensky HL: Family life cycle, work, and the quality of life. Reflections on the roots of happiness, despair and indifference in modern society, in Gardell B, Johansson G (eds): *Working Life. A Social Science Contribution to Work Reform.* London, John Wiley & Sons, 1981.

122. Frankenhaeuser M: Coping with stress at work. *Int J Health Serv* 1981;11:491–510.

123. Frankenhaeuser M: Job demands, health and well being. *J Psychosom Res* 1977;21:313–321.

124. Frankenhaeuser M, Johansson G: Stress at work-psychobiological and psychosocial aspects. *Int Rev Appl Psychol.* (In press.)

125. Johansson G: Subjective well being and temporal patterns of sympathetic-adrenal medullary activity. *Biol Psychol* 1976;4: 157–172.

126. Rissler A: Stress reactions at work and after work during a period of quantitative overload. *Ergonomics* 1977;20:13–16.

127. Frankenhaeuser M: Psychoneuroendocrine approaches to the study of emotion as related to stress and coping, in Howe HE, Dienstbier RA (eds): *Nebraska Symposium on Motivation.* Lincoln, University of Nebraska Press, 1979, pp 123–161.

128. World Health Organization: *Report of the First WHO Interdisciplinary Workshop on Psychosocial Factors and Health.* Geneva, World Health Organization, 1976.

129. Walker CR, Guest RH: *Man on the Assembly Line.* Cambridge, Harvard University Press, 1964.

130. Blauner R: *Alienation and Freedom.* Chicago, Chicago University Press, 1964.

131. Zdravomyslov AG, Yadov VA: Effect of vocational distinctions on the attitude to work, in Osipov GV (ed): *Industry and Labor in the USSR.* London, Tavistock Publications, 1966, pp 99–125.

132. Kornhauser A: *Mental Health of the Industrial Worker.* New York, John Wiley & Sons, 1965.

133. Gardell B: *Produktionsteknik och arbetsgladje.* (Technology,

Alienation and Mental Health. A Sociopsychological Study of Industrial Work.) Stockholm PA Council, 1971.

134. Frankenhaeuser M: Psychobiological aspects of life stress, in Levine S, Ursin H (eds): *Coping and Health.* New York, Plenum Press, 1980, pp 203–223.

135. Frankenhaeuser M, Rissler A: Effects of punishment on catecholamine release and efficiency of performance. *Psychopharmacologia* 1970;17:378–390.

136. Lundberg U, Frankenhaeuser M: Psychophysiological reactions to noise as modified by personal control over noise intensity. *Biol Psychol* 1978;6:51–59.

137. Lundberg U, Frankenhaeuser M: Pituitary-adrenal and sympathetic adrenal correlates of distress and effort. *J Psychosom Res* 1980;24:125–130.

138. Frankenhaeuser M, Lundberg U, Forsman L: Dissociation between sympathetic-adrenal and pituitary-adrenal responses to an achievement situation characterized by high controllability. Comparison between Type A and Type B males and females. *Biol Psychol* 1980;10:79–91.

139. Frankenhaeuser M: The sympathetic-adrenal and pituitary-adrenal response to challenge: comparison between the sexes, in Dembroski TM, Schmidt TH, Blümchen G (eds): *Biobehavioral Bases of Coronary Heart Disease.* Basel, S Karger, 1983, pp 91–105.

140. Levi L: Psykiska Förhälladen i arbetsmiljön Inverkan på hälsa och välbefinnande. (Psychosocial conditions in the work environment. Effects on health and well being.) Arbetsmiljöutredningens betankande, SOU, 1976;3(suppl 2):87–118.

141. Kornlund J: *Demokrati utan Makt.* (Democracy without Power.) Stockholm, Prisma, 1974.

142. Kjellgren O: *Loneadministrativa Utredningen.* (Wage Administrative Study.) Stockholm, LKAB, 1975.

143. Domanverket/Swedish Forest Service: Ettårsrapport: Månadslöne-försöket. Korpilombolo revir (One-year report on experiment with monthly salaries in logging.) Stockholm, Domanverket, Mimeograph, Nov. 13, 1975.

144. SCA-tidningen. Månadslön i skogen. (Monthly salaries in logging.) Sundsvall, Sweden, 1975, No 10.

145. Levi L: The stress of everyday work as reflected in productiveness, subjective feelings, and urinary output of adrenaline and noradrenaline under salaried and piece-work conditions. *J Psychosom Res* 1964;8:199–202.

146. Poyhonen M: Urkkapalka ja Stressi. (Piece-rates and stress.)

Helsingfors Finland, Institut for Arbetshygien, report No. 115, 1975.

147. Bainbridge L: The process controller, in Singelton WT (ed): *The Study of Real Skill.* London, MIT Press, 1978.

148. Johansson G, Gardell B: Psykosociala Aspekter pa processoperatorens arbete. (Psychosocial aspects of process control.) Report, Psykologiska institutionen, University of Stockholm, 1978.

149. Broadbent DE: *Decision and Stress.* New York, Academic Press, 1971.

150. Froberg JE, Karlsson C-G, Levi L, et al: Circadian rhythms of catecholamine excretion, shooting range performance and self-ratings of fatigue during sleep deprivation. *Biol Psychol* 1975;2:175–188.

151. Frankenhaeuser M: The human factor–an obstacle to safe nuclear power. Viewpoint, Stockholm, Mimeograph, 1980.

152. Frankenhaeuser M: To err is human. Biological and psychological aspects of human functioning. *Opuscula Medica.* In press.

153. Johansson G, Aronsson G: Stress reactions in computerized administrative work. *J Occup Behav* 1984;5:159–181.

154. Lundberg U: Urban commuting: Crowdedness and catecholamine excretion. *J Human Stress* 1976;2:26–32.

155. Singer JE, Lundberg U, Frankenhaeuser M: Stress on the train: A study of urban commuting, in Baum A, Singer JE, Valins S (eds): *Advances in Environmental Psychology.* Hillsdale, New Jersey, Erlbaum, 1978, vol 1, pp 41–56.

156. Kagan AR, Cederblad M, Höök B, et al: Evaluation of the effect of increasing the number of nurses on health and behavior of 3 year old children in day care, satisfaction of their parents and health and satisfaction of their nurses. Reports from the Laboratory for Clinical Stress Research, Stockholm, No. 89, 1978.

157. Meissner M: The long arm of the job. A study of work and leisure. *Indust Relations* 1971;10:238–260.

158. Westlander G: Arbetets villkor och fritidens innehåll. (Working conditions and the content of leisure.) Stockholm, Swedish Council for Personal Administration, 1976.

159. Akerstedt T, Levi L: Circadian rhythms in the secretion of cortisol, adrenaline and noradrenaline. *Eur J Clin Invest* 1978;8: 57–58.

160. Levi L: *Stress in Industry. Causes, Effects and Prevention.* Geneva, International Labour Office, 1984.

161. Åkerstedt T, Fröberg JE: Shift work and health-interdisciplinary aspects, in Rentos PG, Shaphard RD (eds): *Shift Work and*

Health, A Symposium. Washington, U.S. Dept of Health, Education, and Welfare, publication No. (NIOSH) 76-203, 1976.

162. Åkerstedt T: Altered sleep/wake patterns and circadian rhythms. Laboratory and field studies of sympathoadrenomedullary and related variables. *Acta Physiol Scand (Suppl)* 469, 1979.

163. Åkerstedt T, Knutsson A, Alfredsson L, Theorell T: Shift work and cardiovascular disease. *Scand J Work Environ Health* 1984;10:409–414.

164. Froberg JE, Karlsson C-G, Levi L, Lidberg L: Psychobiological circadian rhythms during a 73 hour vigil. *Forsvarsmedicin* 1975;11:192–201.

165. Froberg JE: Twenty-four hour patterns in human performance, subjective and physiological variables and differences between morning and evening active subjects. *Biol Psychol* 1977;5: 119–134.

166. Åkerstedt T, Froberg JE: Psychophysiological circadian rhythms in females during 75 hours of sleep deprivation with continuous activity. *Waking Sleeping* 1977;4:387–394.

167. Theorell T, Åkerstedt T: Day and night work: Changes in cholesterol, uric acid, glucose and potassium in serum and in circadian patterns of urinary catecholamine excretion: A longitudinal crossover study of railway workers. *Acta Med Scand* 1976;200:47–53.

168. Åkerstedt T, Torsvall L: Experimental changes in shift schedules–their effects on well being, in Rutenfranz J, Colquhoun P, Kauth P (eds): *Proceedings of the Fourth Symposium on Night and Shift Work*, 1977.

169. Åkerstedt T, Torsvall L: Medical, psychological and social aspects of shift work at the special steel mills in Soderfors. (Swedish). Reports from the laboratory for Clinical Stress Research, University of Stockholm, No. 6, 1977.

170. Åkerstedt T, Torsvall L: Experimental changes in shift schedules–their effects on well being. *Ergonomics* 1978;21:849–856.

171. Olivegård-Landén R, Olsson-Vikstrom A, Oberg B: Ordningspolisen i Stockholm. Delrapport III: 1. Intervention–sociala och psykologiska reaktioner på förändrade arbetstiden. Stockholm, Laboratory for Clinical Stress Research, Karolinska Institute, Report No. 126, 1985.

172. Orth-Gomér K: Ordningspolisen i Stockholm. Delrapport III: 2. Ett försök till intervention mot riskindikatorer for hjärtkärlsjudkom genom förbättrade shiftarbetsbetingelser. Stockholm, Laboratory for Clinical Research, Karolinska Institute, Report No. 127, 1981.

226

173. Ribbing E: Oregelbunda och obekväma arbetstider. Statistika centralbyrån. Stockholm, Utredningsinstitutet, 1974.
174. Thelle D, Rorde OH, Try K, et al: The Tromsø Heart Study. Methods and main results of the cross sectional study. *Acta Med Scand* 1976;200:107–118.
175. Gardell B: Reactions at work and their influence on non-work activities. *Human Relations* 1976;29:855.
176. Karasek RA: *The Impact Of the Work Environment on Life Outside the Job.* Thesis, Boston, MIT Press, 1976.
177. Marmot MG, Rose G, Shipley M, et al: Employment grade and coronary heart disease in British civil servants. *J Epidemiol Commun Health* 1978;32:241–249.
178. Puska P, Mustaniemi H: Incidence and presentation of myocardial infarction in North Karelia, Finland. *Acta Med Scand* 1975;197:211–216.
179. Antonowsky A: Social class and the major cardiovascular diseases. *J Chron Dis* 1968;21:65–106.
180. Lehman EW: Social class and coronary heart disease. A sociological assessment of the medical literature. *J Chron Dis* 20: 381–391.
181. Holme I, Helgeland A, Hjermann I, et al: Coronary risk factors in various occupational groups. The Oslo Study. *Br J Prev Soc* 1977;31:96–100.
182. Orth-Gomer K: Psychological stress and ischemic heart disease in Stockholm and New York. *J Psychosom Res* 1979;23: 165–173.
183. Hinkle LE, Whitney LH, Lehman EW, et al: Occupation, education and coronary heart disease. *Science* 1968;161:238.
184. Frankenhaeuser M, Myrsten A-L, Wasak M, et al: Dosage and time effects of cigarette smoking. *Psychopharmacol* 1968;13: 311.
185. Haynes RB, Sackett DL, Taylor DW: Increased absenteeism from work after detection and labeling of hypertensive patients. *N Engl J Med* 1978;14:741.
186. Nirkko O, Lauroma M, Siltanen P, et al: Psychological risk factors related to coronary heart disease. Prospective studies among policemen in Helsinki. *Acta Med Scand* 1982;660:137.
187. Shekelle RB, Schneider AS, Lin SC, et al: Work tension and risk of coronary heart disease (CHD). *Am Heart Assoc CVD Epidemiol Newsletter* 1979;26:66.
188. Kittel F, Kornitzer M, Dramaix M: Coronary heart disease and job stress in two cohorts of bank clerks. *Psychother Psychosom* 1980;34:110.

189. Theorell T, Flodérus-Myrhed B: "Workload" and risk of myocardial infarction–a prospective psychosocial analysis. *Inst J Epidemiol* 1977;6:17–21.

190. Theorell T, Rahe RH: Behavior and life satisfactions characteristic of Swedish subjects with myocardial infarction. *J Chronic Dis* 1972;25:139.

191. Sales SM, House J: Job dissatisfaction as a possible factor in coronary heart disease. *J Chronic Dis* 1971;23:861.

192. Schaefer H, Blohmke M: *Herzkrankheit durch psychosozialen Stress.* Heidelberg, Hüthig, 1977.

193. Theorell T, Flodérus B, Lind E: The relationship of disturbing life-changes and emotions to the early development of myocardial infarction and other serious illness. *Int J Epidemiol* 1975; 4:281.

194. Flodérus B: Psychosocial factors in relation to coronary heart disease and associated risk factors. *Nordisk Hygienisk tidskrift Suppl* 1974;6.

195. Caplan RD, Cobbs S, French JR, et al: Job demands and worker health: Main effects and occupational differences. Washington, US Department of Health, Education, and Welfare, publication No. (NIOSH) 75-160, 1975.

196. Cooper CL, Marshall J: Occupational sources of stress: A review of the literature relating to coronary heart disease and mental ill health. *J Occup Psychol* 1976;49:11.

197. Chesney MA, Sevelius G, Black GW, et al: Work environment, type A behavior and coronary heart disease factors. *J Occup Med* 1981;23:551.

198. Dembroski TM, McDougall JM, Shields JL: Physiologic reactions to social challenge in persons evidencing the type A coronary-prone behavior pattern. *J Human Stress* 1977;3:2.

199. Aronsson G, Barklöv K: Att arbeta inom lokaltrafiken. Arbetsförhållanden-hälsa-fritid. Forskargruppen för arbetslivets socialpsykologi. Psykologiska institutionen, University of Stockholm, report No. 26, 1980.

200. Johansson G, Aronsson G, Lindström BO: Socialpsykologiska och fysiologiska stressreaktion i högmekaniserat arbete. Psykologiska institutionen, University of Stockholm, report No. 7, 1976.

201. Timio M, Gentili S: Adrenosympathetic overactivity under conditions of work stress. *Br J Prev Soc Med* 1976;3:262.

202. Cochrane R: Neuroticism and the discovery of high blood pressure. *J Psychosom Res* 1969;13:21.

203. Karasek RA, Schnall P, Schwartz J, et al: *Psychosocial Char-*

acteristics of Occupations in Relation to Blood Pressure. A study of two national random samples of American working men. Stencil, Department of Industrial Engineering and Operations Research, Columbia University, New York, 1982.

204. Arbetsmiljö, levnadsförhållanden. Stockholm, Swedish Central Bureau of Statistics, Report No. 32, 1982.

205. Karasek RA, Russel RS, Theorell T: Physiology of stress and regeneration in job related cardiovascular illness. *J Human Stress* 1982;8:29.

206. Johansson G: Individual control in a repetitive task. Effects on performance, effort and physiological arousal. Psykologiska institutionen, University of Stockholm, report No. 579, 1981.

207. Johansson G, Aronsson G: *Stress Reactions in Computerized Administrative Work.* Reports from the Department of Psychology, University of Stockholm, suppl 50, 1980.

208. Karasek RA: Job demands, job decision latitude and mental strain: Implications for job redesign. *Admin Sci Qtly* 1979; 24:285.

209. Selye J, Bajusz E: Conditioning by corticoids for the production of cardiac lesions with noradrenaline. *Acta Endocrinol* 1959;30:183.

210. Alfredsson L, Karasek RA, Theorell T: Myocardial infarction risk and psychosocial work environment: An analysis of the male Swedish working force. *Soc Sci Med* 1982;16:463–467.

211. Alfredsson L, Spetz C-L, Theorell T: Type of occupation and near-future hospitalization for myocardial infarction and some other diagnoses. *Int J Epidemiol,* September 1985.

212. Karasek RA, Theorell T, Schwartz J, et al: *Job Characteristics of Occupations in Relation to the Prevalence of Myocardial Infarction in the US HES and the US HANES.* Department of Industrial Engineering and Operations Research, Columbia University, New York, 1982.

213. Alfredsson L, Theorell T: Psykosocial arbetsmiljo och hjärtinfarkt-risk. *Läkartidningen* 1982;79:4658.

214. Karasek RA, Baker D, Marxer F, et al: Job decision latitude, job demands and cardiovascular disease. A prospective study of Swedish men. *Am J Public Health* 1981;71:694.

215. Karasek RA, Theorell T, Schwartz J, et al: Job, psychological factors and coronary heart disease. *Adv Cardiol* 1982;29:62–67.

216. Alfredsson L, Theorell T: Job characteristics of occupations and myocardial infarction risk—effect of possible confounding factors. *Soc Sci Med* 1983;17:1497–1503.

217. Littler WA, West MJ, Honour AJ, et al: The variability of arterial pressure. *Am Heart J* 1978;95:180–189.
218. Harshfield GA, Pickering TG, Laragh JH: A validation study of the Del Mar Avionics ambulatory blood pressure system. *Ambulatory Electrocardiol* 1979;1:7–12.
219. Harshfield GA, Pickering TG, Kleinert HD, et al: Situational variations of blood pressure in ambulatory hypertensive patients. *Psychosom Med* 1982;44:237–245.
220. Sokolow M, Werdegar D, Kain HK, et al: Relationship between level of blood pressure measured casually and by portable recorders and severity of complications in essential hypertension. *Circulation* 1966;34:279–292.
221. Jason M, Devereux R, Borer JS, et al: Twenty-four hour arterial pressure measurement. Improved prediction of left ventricular dysfunction in essential hypertension, abstract. *J Am Coll Cardiol* 1983;1:599.
222. Favazza AR, Thompson JJ: Social networks of alcoholics: Some early findings. *Alcoholism* 1984;8:9–15.
223. Webster's New Collegiate Dictionary. Springfield, Mass, G & C Merriam Co, 1981, p 1143.
224. Comfort A: Alcohol as a social drug and health hazard. *Lancet* 1984;1:443–444.
225. West LJ, Maxwell DS, Noble EP, et al: Alcoholism, UCLA Conference. *Ann Intern Med* 1984;100:405–416.
226. Alcoholism study seeks answer to growing problem, editorial. *Am Fam Physician* 1983;27:186–190.
227. Hollermann S, Burchell A: *The Cost of Alcohol Misuse.* London, Department of Health and Social Security, Government Economic Service working paper No 37, 1981.
228. Alcoholic disease, editorial. *Lancet* 1982;1:1105–1106.
229. Shlapentokn V: In Soviet, women emerge superior. *New York Times* section 1, Feb 4, 1984, p 23.
230. Hogberg CH: The Soviet Union: Losing the battle of the bottle. *Alcoholism: The National Magazine* 1984;4:58–61.
231. Brenton M: *Help For the Troubled Employee.* Public Affairs Pamphlet No. 511. New York, The Public Affairs Committee, Inc, 1982, pp 2–3.
232. An employer's policy on alcohol use. Center City, Minn, Hazelden, 1981, p 7.
233. Whyte AJ: Evaluating EAPs effectiveness in the workplace. *Alcoholism: The National Magazine* 1984;4:25–31.
234. Wrich JT: *The Employee Assistance Program: Updated For The 1980's.* Center City, Minn, Hazelden, 1980, pp 22–23.

235. Geller A: *Alcohol and Anxiety.* Minneapolis, Johnson Institute Inc, 1983, p 15.
236. Gitlow SE: *A Pharmacological Approach to Alcoholism.* New York, AA Grapevine, 1968, pp 312–327.
237. Blair BR: Emotions which permit supervisory enabling, in *Supervisors and Managers as Enablers.* Minneapolis, Johnson Institute Inc, 1983, pp 11–12.
238. Naisbitt J: *Megatrends, From An Industrial To An Information Society.* New York, Warner Books Inc, 1982, pp 1–33.
239. Lewis CS: *Out of the Silent Planet.* New York, Macmillan Publishing Co Inc, 1965, p 42.
240. Meagher RC, Sieber F, Spivak JL: Suppression of hematopoietic-progenitor-cell proliferation by ethanol and acetaldehyde. *N Engl J Med* 1982;307:845–849.
241. Fox R: *Imagine Such A Disease.* New York, AA Grapevine, 1968, p 27.
242. Jaffe AJ: *The Retirement Dilemma, Industrial Gerontology Studies on Problems of Work and Age.* The National Council on Aging, Summer, 1972.
243. Romano D: *I've Got to Work Till I Die.* New York, Vantage Press, 1965.
244. Harris L: *The Myth and Reality of Aging in America,* Washington, National Council of the Aging, Inc, Nov 1974.
245. Woodring P: *Saturday Review,* Aug 7, 1976.
246. Allman DB: The Right to be Useful. Speech delivered at the AMA Aging Conference, Boston, Sept 17, 1969.
247. Osleeb J: Task force reports on problems and needs of older workers, in *The World at Boston University* 1984;4:1–3.
248. United Nations Statistical Yearbook and Demographic Yearbook.
249. Vital Statistics of the US National Center for Health Statistics, US Dept of Health, Education, and Welfare, Public Health Service, Rockville, MD, 1980.
250. Population Estimates and Projections; Current population reports. US Bureau of Census.
251. Coyle JT, Price DL, DeLong MR: Brain mechanisms in Alzheimer's disease. *Hosp Pract* 17;55–63.
252. Harris L: Pleasant retirement expected. *Washington Post,* Nov 28, 1965.
253. Tibbitts C, Donahue W (eds): *Social and Psychological Aspects of Aging.* New York, Columbia University Press, 1962.
254. Chesney MA, Sevelius G, Black GW, et al: Work environment, type A behavior and coronary heart disease risk factors. *J Occup Med* 1981;23(8):551–555.

255. Sevelius G: *Stress Management, Step 5 – Minimizing Your Risk of Heart Attack, Possibly An Unnecessary Disease.* Santa Clara, California, Health and Safety Publications, 1981.
256. Rehabilitation Act of 1973, Section 503.
257. *Health/PAC Bull* May/June 1980 at 13.
258. *Arch Environ Health* 412 (1975) at 414.
259. *Am Jur* 2d *Master and Servant* §§ 125,126
260. 16 *ALR* 3d 564 at 569.
261. *Am J Public Health* 381(1973) at 382.
262. *Lotspeich v Chance Vought Aircraft,* 369 SW 2d 705 at 709-10 (Tex).
263. *Hoover v Williamson,* 203 A 2d 861 at 863, 236 Md 250 (1964).
264. 69 *ALR* 2d 1213 at 1215.
265. *Ford v Louisiana & A.R. Co* 196 So 403 (1940). 16 *ALR* 3d 564 at 618.
266. 10 *ALR* 3d 1071 at 1073.
267. *Larson, Law of Workman's Compensation* §72.64 at 14-217-218.
268. 53 *Ind LJ* 585 at 594 (1978).
269. 9 *Hofstra LR* 665 at 672 (1981).
270. 53 *Ind LJ* 585 at 596 (1978).
271. 9 *Hofstra LR* 665 at 677 (1981).
272. *Larson, Law of Worker's Compensation* §45.32 (c).
273. *Duprey v Shane,* 249, p 218, 39 Cal 2n 781 (1952).
274. *Ind LJ* 585 at 593-6 (1978).
275. 63 *Am J Public Health* 381 at 383 1973.
276. 127 *ALR* 1108 at 1109.
277. *Smith v Mallinckrodt* 251 SW 155,212 Mo App 158 (1923).
278. *Owens v Atlantic Coast Lumber Corp* 94 SE 15,108 SC 258 (1917).
279. 21 *ALR* 3d 1066 at 1071.
280. 21 *ALR* 3d 845 at 880-1.
281. *Walker v Von Wedel,* 237, p 86, 108 Okla 292 (1925).
282. *Johns-Manville, etc v Contra Costa, etc,* 612 p 2d 948, 165 *Cal Rptr*
283. 26 *ATLA LR* August 1983, 247–250.
284. Peters T, Waterman P: *In Search of Excellence. Lessons From America's Best Run Companies.* New York, Harper & Row, 1982.
285. Kahn R, Wolfe D, Dunn R, et al: *Organizational Stress.* New York, John Wiley & Sons, 1964.
286. Holmes T, Rahe R: The social readjustment rating scale. *J Psychosom Res* 1967;1:213–218.
287. Seamonds B: Stress factors and their effect on absenteeism in a corporate employee group. *J Occup Med* 1982;24:393–397.

288. Weiman C: A study of occupational stressors and the evidence of disease/risk. *J Occup Med* 1977;17:119–122.
289. Pellegrino J, Seamonds B: Managing stress is good business. Washington, National Mental Health Association, 1982.
290. Ross WD: *Practical Psychiatry for Industrial Physicians.* Springfield, Ill, Charles C Thomas Publisher, 1956.
291. Wolf S, Goodell H: *Behavioral Science in Clinical Medicine.* Springfield, Ill, Charles C Thomas Publisher, 1976.
292. Gherman EM: *Stress and The Bottom Line.* New York, AMACOM, 1981.
293. Bureau of National Affairs, Washington: *Personnel Policies Forum Survey* 1981;132:3–11.
294. Selye H: *The Stress of Life.* New York, McGraw-Hill Book Co, 1956.
295. Knippel G: The survivor's checklist. *J Trans Anal* 1980;10:61–67.
296. Moss L: *Management Stress.* Reading, Massachusetts, Addison-Wesley Publishing Co, Inc, 1981.
297. Greiff B, Munter P: *Trade-offs.* New York, New American Library, 1980.
298. Brodman K, Hellman LP: The relation of group morale to the incidence and duration of medical incapacity in industry. *Psychosom Med* 1947;9:381–385.
299. McLean A: *Occupational Stress.* Springfield, Ill, Charles C Thomas Publisher, 1974.
300. Matsumoto YS: Social stress and coronary heart disease in Japan: A hypothesis. *Millbank Mem Fund Q* 1970;48:9–36.
301. Wolf S: Psychosomatic aspects of industrial medicine. *South Med J* 1955;4:79.
302. Ripley HS, Wolf S: Data concerning adaptation to the isolated situation of a combat zone in the Southwest Pacific. *J Nerv Ment Dis* 1951;114:234.
303. Weider A: Some aspects of an industrial mental hygiene program. *J Appl Psychol* 1951;35:383–385.
304. Fielding JE: Effectiveness of employee health improvement programs. *J Occup Med* 1982;24:11.
305. Seidman LS, Sevelius G, Ewald P: A cost-effectiveness weight loss program at the worksite. *J Occup Med* 1984;26:10.
306. Barnett GO: The application of computer-based medical record systems in ambulatory practice. *N Engl J Med* 1984;310:1643–1650.
307. Taylor CB, Agras WS, Sevelius G: *Managing Hypertension in the Workplace.* New York, John Wiley and Sons, 1985.

308. Nelkin D: Workers at risk. *Science* 1983;222:125.
309. Fletcher BC, Payne RL: Stress at Work. A preview and theoretical framework. Parts 1 and 2. *Personnel Behav* 1980;1: 19–29;2:5–8.
310. *Physicians for the 21st Century.* Report of the Panel on the General Professional Education of the Physicians and College Preparation for Medicine, AAMC, 1984.

INDEX

DATE DUE

MR 14 '97			
MR 31 '97			

Demco, Inc. 38-293